Binder of Wounds

Binder
of
Wounds

A Medley of Meditations

Essence
PUBLISHING

Belleville, Ontario, Canada

*B*inder of *W*ounds
A Medley of Meditations

Copyright © 1996, Sini Den Otter

The Scripture quotations contained herein are from the *New Revised Standard Version* of the Bible (Copyright © 1993 and 1989 by the Division of Christian Education of the National Council of the Churches of Christ in the U.S.A. Used by permission. All rights reserved.)

ISBN: 1-896400-07-8

Essence Publishing is a Christian Book Publisher dedicated to furthering the work of Christ through the written word. For more information, contact: 103B Cannifton Rd., Belleville, ON, Canada K8N 4V2.
Phone: 1-800-238-6376. Fax: (613) 962-3055.
Email: essence@intranet.on.ca

Printed in Canada
by

Essence
PUBLISHING

*To Job
and all our children*

Table of Contents

Preface. 9

1. The Formation of Ministry 11
2. The Church. 16
3. Driving in the Fog. 21
4. The Lord is My Shepherd 24
5. Walk and Not Be Weary 27
6. The Answer is Yes. 29
7. Prophetesses 31
8. The Aroma of Christ 34
9. Land of Forgetfulness. 36
10. A Time for Grieving 38
11. Grief for a Baby 41
12. Mother's Day. 43
13. Flowers 45
14. The Everlasting Arms. 47
15. Home. 50
16. Living Letters 53
17. Hope Returns 56
18. Morning by Morning New Mercies I See . 59
19. Binder of Wounds 61
20. An Anniversary. 66

21. A Renewed Focus 69
22. A New Assignment 71
23. Reconnecting. 73
24. Facing the Truth. 75
25. Friendship. 78
26. Joy and Sorrow 80
27. A Complete Bible 83
28. Fear. 86
29. Spiritual Wellness. 89
30. Defeated 92
31. Dreams 95
32. Random Acts of Kindness 98
33. Thanksgiving 101
34. Giving 104
35. Where Have All the Women Gone? 106
36. Counting Our Days 110
37. We Are Jesus' Friends 113
38. Darkness 117
39. Memorial Services. 119
40. Playfulness 122
41. Burning Hearts 125

Bibliography 131

Preface

*T*his is a book about God and God's dealings with God's people. It is my desire that the reader will be touched and inspired by these stories and will trust God to lead, knowing that He never forces, but rather powerfully encourages us to follow His voice. I hope you will be able to sense the wonder of God's provision and guidance in my journey towards becoming a hospital chaplain.

> *I am confident of this, that the one who began a good work among you will bring it to completion by the day of Jesus Christ.*
> Philippians 1:6

The first two chapters of the book describe how this "work" all started in my life, since many people have asked me why I chose this ministry. The rest of the book contains some of my experiences in the chaplaincy, in the hope that even one person may be encouraged by them. I have changed names and circumstances to maintain confidentiality.

I thank my husband Job for his patience and encouragement in the long process of achieving my goals and writing these meditations. I also want to thank all those who have supported me in the process of obtaining endorsement for my work as a chaplain: the people of my local church, Classis Alberta North and the Chaplain Committee of the Christian Reformed Church. And I want to thank those who have supported me in times of discouragement and those who have offered to be prayer partners. I believe that God provided people to be there at the right time and the right place — people who believe that what I am doing is God's work and that it is worthy of their support. You are God's gift to me.

Sini Den Otter
Edmonton, 1996

1

The Formation of Ministry

Do not neglect the gift that is in you....
1 Timothy 4:14

These words were spoken by the apostle Paul to Timothy, a young Christian, who became a companion to Paul in his missionary work. Paul gave Timothy advice on how to be a good servant of Jesus Christ and also told him not to neglect the gift for ministry that was in him. With this spiritual gift came also the responsibility to use it and not let it go to waste. Any gift, such as painting, writing or mathematical skills, that has been given to people needs to be developed and practiced. But when God gives people the gift for ministry, it is special because it promises life for both the present and for the future. Therefore, this list of instructions is quite long — awesome actually — because it is a unique gift that has been given for the special purpose of saving those who hear the message. That message of God's love may be heard in many ways, sometimes not in words, but in deeds of kindness, in forgiveness or simply by the presence of another person.

The gift for a particular ministry is inherent in a person and the formation of it is influenced by events and people who cross their paths. I can certainly trace the events in my life that led up to the work I now do as a chaplain. I was a child when the second World War broke out. Living in Rotterdam, the Netherlands, which was bombed severely, I learned to be fearful of fire and danger and to pray for safekeeping, for food, for protection, and for our family to stay together. I became an immigrant when I went with my husband to Canada and I experienced loneliness and homesickness. These feelings have never completely left me.

I became a wife and mother of four children and the blessings of raising a family were mine along with many new insights. The empty nest was another stage at which time feelings of uselessness and "what now?" were prevalent, until a focus away from family helped me to look beyond that stage in my life.

A depression resulted from a number of factors and I experienced despair and darkness without being able to see a speck of light or hope. The greatest regret I have about this is that it happened during the teenage years of my children and that they were deprived of a happy home environment during those years. Now that all four of our children are married, we are blessed with sons-in-law, a daughter-in-law and grandchildren. Distance from each other has created a special bond of missing each other and making the most of the times that we are able to spend together.

My depression was a time of searching for direction and what God wanted me to be and do. The seeds for ministry that had always been there began to develop. We went to see the film, *The Hiding Place*, by Corrie ten Boom. Because the film was made in Holland, I could relate to the story, the setting, the events and the people. Corrie and her family offered shelter to a number of Jews during World War II. The Jews were targeted as undesirable by the Nazis and were to report to them. As a result, many Jews went into hiding in private homes such as the ten Boom's. However, this family was betrayed by some people down the street and Corrie and her sister were taken to a concentration camp in Germany. The film showed this camp in Ravensbruck where conditions were terrible. Corrie went from bunk to bunk to comfort the other prisoners. Out of her strong faith commitment, Corrie conducted worship and witnessed miracles. These miracles were often such that they were only recognized later, after the fact. Corrie writes: "Because of the bugs which infested our barrack, the women guards and officers kept their distance, and we were able to hold our Bible studies without fear. God had a use for the vermin, after all." [1]

While watching that film, I "knew" that some day I would do this kind of work — bedside ministry. The experiences of my life became valuable tools for relating to people in need. Another experience was added when I learned that I had a cancerous tumor in the thyroid gland. I had worked only one year as a chaplain after years of study and training, and I questioned God as to the timing. "Why now when I just got started?" But I recovered and have been working since, now being able to relate to patients who go through surgery and test after test, waiting for results.

As I reflect on the last ten years of ministry in active treatment, I have been richly blessed. I have been able to be with people in a variety of ways, with the dying and with families of patients who came to emergency in cases of trauma. I have been with cancer patients who went through tremendous suffering before God took them home. There were many rich and profound experiences, but there were also dry times when I thought, "Why am I here?"

Over the years, I have been with many young couples who suffered the loss of a child through still-birth or miscarriage. Again, having experienced this grief in my family of origin serves me well. I still remember the sorrow when my parents suffered the loss of a baby and the guilt my mother felt. When I went back to Holland just a few years ago, it all of a sudden struck me that I could have had another sister, besides the two sisters and two brothers I have now. This goes to show how many facets this sort of grief has. Out of that experience I am able to be with these young people and give them comfort and practical help.

All of these events in my life have been a rich source for the ministry of presence with patients, and it amazes me how God is using these for good. Even when I do not remember certain patients or their family members, they remember what it meant to them to have someone there in their time of need. Even my Dutch accent (which I often resent) serves as a bridge sometimes with people who come from other countries. I can feel for the many women from different cultures who come to our hospital to give birth. Often young women have been in Canada only a short time and have difficulty expressing their needs, and I try to reassure them. I remember a young native woman who was so shy and withdrawn that it was painful to watch. A nurse had been impatient with her when she tried to feed her baby. The new mother gave me a piece of paper with her complaints about this. She asked, "Is it because I am native?" I looked at her young son who was sleeping peacefully in his bassinet, and I told her that I thought that she was a good mother and I was sure she would do well. I think that did more for her than what the nurse had said, although she meant well. I thought about the time when our first daughter was born and how alone and frightened I was. At that time, husbands were not allowed to be present at birth and we did not have the benefit of pre-natal classes. I, as a very inexperienced mother, would have benefited from some positive input.

Although the difficulties were very hard to take when I was in the middle of them, they were nevertheless opportunities for learning which God is using for good. Many times I am reminded that *all things work together for good for those who love God* (Rom. 8:28). If I had not been depressed, I would not have searched so hard for direction in my life and my faith would not have been deepened and tested. God has led my life in a direction that I had never dreamed possible. I'll speak more about that in the next chapter.

---

[1]Corrie ten Boom, *Each New Day* (Minneapolis: World Wide Publications, 1977), November 27.

2
The Church

For the gifts and the calling of God are irrevocable.
Romans 11:29

"This mysterious depth of the ground plan
and human potential allows room for the Creator
to act within the unconscious
long before this activity breaks into consciousness....
Through the energizing presence of the Holy One,
spontaneous images break the silence
of consciousness, capture our attention, inspire
visions of the future and lure each of us
toward human fulfillment and the fulfillment
of the eternal purpose of God."[2]

J believe God's call was always there, but it only came into consciousness when I was ready for it. And even then I would not believe it and it took a long time before I could entertain that call and embrace it to the fullest. The struggle for clarity for the future went on during my depression. The children were maturing and I found myself with time on my hands and the need to do something meaningful. I enrolled in University and graduated with a Bachelor of Arts degree in Sociology and Religious Studies. When I expressed the wish to study theology, I surprised myself. I had just said something that I was not even aware of and that came out of the unconscious into consciousness. That's how God works. God shapes and prepares our lives to fulfill a purpose that He has prepared for us.

After graduating, I searched again for direction. What does one do with a B.A.? I took a job as church secretary and during that time something else surfaced. I said to my pastor, "I want to become a chaplain." This thought had never entered my mind before either, but it had been there deep in the recesses of my being, shaped by such events as the war, the movie, *The Hiding Place,* and a sermon I had heard as a teenager. I'll never forget that powerful preacher who brought us the joy of freedom in Jesus Christ. One Sunday he preached on being heirs of the kingdom. "We are all children of the King," he said, "hold your heads high because we are royalty." I remember thinking, "That's me too." This was long before I even knew there was a women's issue and how painful this would become for me. I did not know, of course, what this early stirring would lead to, but, in retrospect, I know that God was doing the preparatory work for this ministry to the sick and hurting.

When the idea of becoming a chaplain was brought from deep down into consciousness, it stayed there for a while, as if it had to sink in. It did sink in for about half a year until things came together and I was accepted into the first unit of Clinical Pastoral Education. This is a program where the student does the actual work of visiting the sick, as well as studying theory and doing groupwork. The aim is for the student to learn about him or herself, what values and attitudes he or she holds and to deal with any problems there may be. This is done in a group and under individual supervision. To apply for C.P.E., I had to submit several written documents, including an autobiography. I wrote about my impressions of many events as a child during the war. Following that, my supervisor assigned me to a burn unit so that I could work through any feelings of fear, anger or remnants of trauma. It was as if God was saying, "If you want to do this kind of work, here you have it." Horrible disfigurement, sick minds, as well as many courageous people were all part of that first unit. Many experiences came my way and how I carried on, I don't know.

At the end of that year, I had to make a choice of whether to continue and study theology so that I could become a chaplain, or to do the visiting as a volunteer. Another struggle ensued. Did I really want to go ahead? It became clear that I should. In four years, I completed a Masters of Theological Studies and finished five units of C.P.E. I was certified as a Specialist in Institutional Ministry. My thesis was entitled, "HESED: God's everlasting love expressed in baptism invites men and women to a mutuality in ministry."

In order to qualify for certification with CAPPE (Canadian Association for Pastoral Practice and Education), I needed ordination or endorsement from a denomination. When I started on this course, I was not aware of the implications for the Christian Reformed Church. A chaplain traditionally is a male ordained minister of the Word and Sacraments and, in 1988, no progress had been made towards the ordination of women. Through a long process of applications to the local, regional and international (U.S. and Canada) boards, I was finally endorsed by the Chaplain Committee of the Christian

Reformed Church. In the local church, I was ordained as a deacon at large with the special task of doing chaplaincy work. I needed this official position in order to be accountable to a faith community. Shortly after this important step, I obtained a chaplain position at an active treatment hospital in Edmonton. This hospital opened as an active treatment hospital in 1988 and, in 1995, it changed into a Community Health Centre, due to cutbacks in funding from the government.

This whole process has not been easy, since I was the first woman in the Christian Reformed Church to go this route. But God led the way and made it all come to pass. I have felt supported by many, especially on the official levels. But people on the grassroots level have not always been in favour of what was happening. I often had to go ahead without the approval of people who meant so much to me; I had to go on without them. I learned that God wants those whom He calls to depend on His leading more than on the approval of others. Another struggle that was hard to work through was fought on an internal level. It took a long time before I could even say out loud that I was a chaplain. The ideas that seem to limit the freedom that we have in Jesus Christ were very much ingrained in me, and it took conscious effort to break away from them.

Was it worth the struggle, inwardly and outwardly? I believe so, although it has taken its toll. In the beginning, someone advised me to let others do the fighting for me. It was good advice, but I have come into my own to such an extent that I can better carry my own torch. I need a support system, of course, and I cannot function without prayer partners, but I do feel stronger and more confident to speak out. And I continue to encourage the use of inclusive language and to welcome women and men as equal partners in ministry. I have worked enough with abused women to be deeply grieved by the disrespect shown to them. Sometimes the human side gives up on dreaming dreams and has difficulty believing that the prophecy of sons and daughters will be heard and honoured, especially in the Church. But I walk on in faith as an heir of the Kingdom, aware of this high calling.

---

[2]B. Campbell Johnson, *Pastoral Spirituality* (Philadelphia: The Westminster Press, 1988) p. 47.

3

Driving in the Fog

I drive but You guide me.
(Spanish prayer)

*J*t happened only once that I was asked to go
to a town about 60 kilometers from Edmonton to conduct a workshop in a rural hospital on behalf of our pastoral care department. I have
been on other out-of-town assignments but there was
always someone else to do the driving. This time I was
on my own and it so happened that there was a dense
fog that day, which is very unusual in our area. I had
never been to this town, so I had to watch for roadsigns
and turns in the road. Since highway driving is not my
forte, I was very uptight about this trip. I prayed for
God to take the fog away; sort of, "Let the sun come
through please, God." I was tense as the fog seemed to
get heavier instead of lighter. "Exactly on the day that I
have to drive 60 kilometers out of town, there has to be
this fog," I muttered.

God did not perform a miracle, but instead I heard a
still small voice saying, "I have given you driving skills."
It was very clear as I repeated this out loud to make it
my own. Yes! I have driving skills. I needed to hear that.
I arrived safely, and in the afternoon when I stepped out
of the small hospital, I was sure that the fog would have
lifted. Instead, the fog was still the same, dense and

foreboding. Again, I made my way back carefully, telling myself the whole time that I had driving skills — I needed to encourage myself. I made it home.

That day in the fog taught me a valuable lesson. God does not take away our problems, but God provides us with the means to navigate through them. I often think of the short statement, "I have given you driving skills," when talking to patients or families of patients. Sometimes they ask me to pray for a miracle or for the patient to wake up out of an irreversible coma. People ask for it not to be true when they cannot accept it. They cannot accept the terrible truth that their baby is dead, for instance. It cannot be!

It is very difficult to accept an unacceptable truth, but God in His mercy says, "I have given you survival skills." God does not take the pain away, just like He did not take the fog away. The denial as the first phase of grieving is part of the survival skills. Reality hits gradually, and God in His grace is there in every phase to hold, embrace and comfort.

It is not only in grief that God gives strength to go on. In any difficult situation, God paves the way — but not by doing the work for us or by removing the obstacles. Often in my experience, I have heard the words, "You do it. I have given you my Spirit, now do it." That has not been easy, because walking in the Spirit is maturing in the faith. And maturing brings its growing pains. But if God had cleared the way of all obstacles, my faith would not have been challenged and tested and it would not have matured the way it has. That testing has also affirmed for me the calling I felt to pursue the chaplaincy. That journey has not been free of obstacles from the outside or from the inside. The struggle has at times been almost unbearable and yet God never said that I could give up. It would have been easier in some ways. Yet, I have been blessed beyond expectation and I am still walking by faith. That faith, so closely connected with background, upbringing and individuality, is still being shaped and refined for further service.

4

The Lord is My Shepherd

The LORD is my shepherd, I shall not want.
Psalm 23:1

*M*any people have been comforted by the words of this psalm written by David, the shepherd boy. Its words are so familiar that it speaks to people, whether they are religious or not. As a chaplain, I am often called in by our staff when a patient has passed away. Family members may have been present at the time of death or they were informed after the fact and had come to say their last farewells. I then invite the family to gather around the bed to give thanks for what that person meant to loved ones and friends and to ask God to bless the work of their hands. This brings closure to an event that may have been expected or that may have been sudden, as in the case of an accident. Reading of Scripture and saying a prayer are often the means of putting words to grief, and committing the deceased to God's care and mercy. A prayer is seldom refused under these circumstances. It is a time when people reflect on life and death because it brings them in touch with their own mortality and with eternity.

I remember once being with a dying patient and his wife. She asked me to read Psalm 23 to them. During the reading, the man quietly breathed his last and his wife was very much comforted that he died while these words were being read. "I will always remember these words," she said. "He went so peacefully." There are also people who find comfort in these words because they are associated with dying and funerals. They do not believe in dwelling in the house of the Lord, however. If they have not lived the life of faith, they won't draw strength from it during illness and death. For some, a distant memory of Sunday school stories may be rekindled and renewal of faith may happen. I myself have not witnessed deathbed conversions and it is sad to hear someone refuse to accept the comforting words of the Good News. Yet God is the final decision-maker and only He knows their hearts.

To be present at a deathbed is one thing, but to be there when a doctor breaks the news of a death in the emergency department is another experience. When patients are brought in by ambulance, every effort is made to bring them back to life but this is not always successful. The patient may have suffered a stroke or heart attack, or may have been involved in an accident. The death of a child due to sudden infant death syndrome is the most tragic I have witnessed. The death of young children seems so futile, so cruel, so unbelievable. Words are often not wanted or necessary, but just being there is something a family never forgets. They are confused, distraught and bewildered, not knowing what to do. I have often been there with a steadying hand and a compassionate heart in their time of need. This personal touch reminds people that there is a God who cares — a God who grieves with them and who offers hope in the midst of tragedy.

In one of the Roman Catholic hospitals where I worked, staff and administration are convinced that the spiritual care that is provided by the pastoral care department is crucial to the care we give. The mission statement speaks of respect and dignity for all who come to our institution and even in times of cutbacks we try to be considerate of the patient and to look not only after the physical needs but also after the spiritual and emotional aspects. If a patient feels cared for, healing is helped along and promoted.

As a chaplain, I have to continually be in touch with my own needs — the need to stay in touch with God and to take time for personal devotions and to be recharged. The words of Psalm 23:3a, *[God] restores my soul*, need to be taken to heart and made my own time and again. I need to be restored, because sometimes I am so empty that I cannot give anymore, and only God can supply that new store of grace and mercy to be passed on to those in need.

5
Walk and Not Be Weary

But those who wait for the LORD
shall renew their strength,
they shall mount up with wings like eagles,
they shall run and not be weary,
they shall walk and not faint.
Isaiah 40:31

*W*eariness is certainly part of my life and I sometimes need a shot in the arm to keep on going. Being a listener is hard work. People who think that "just visiting" is not draining have never tried it.

On a cold February afternoon, I forced myself to go for a walk. I walk for exercise and do much thinking while I am walking; actually I have long conversations with God. On this cold afternoon it was –20° C and a brisk wind from the north made it even colder. I had little inclination to go out into the stinging wind and brave what our daughter would call "pins and needles weather." Yet I did go and the walk was so refreshing and renewing that I was reminded of this verse in Isaiah 40. God gives new strength when ours runs out. Some visits are energizing, some are draining. Some patients are a joy to visit and others suck the energy out of me because they are so needy.

One day a nurse asked me to visit a man who was being very difficult and who took his anger out on the staff. I was weary and I thought, "What do you expect me to say or do?" But I did visit and it turned out to be very rewarding. Because I was able to be there and listen, the patient was able to acknowledge his anger, name its source and blow off steam. His concerns were not unreasonable either, when looking at it from his point of view. And as usual when someone finds some sympathy for his cause, the man's anger deflated and he admitted that he had been hard on the nurses. "I better smarten up," he concluded.

It amazed me that somehow I had the strength to be there as a listener. I had taken the time to say a short prayer before entering the room, a simple, "Lord, help me." Just as it took some courage to go out in the cold weather, so it takes courage to keep on asking for strength and to not rely on my own. When I fail to commit my day to God, I am the one who suffers and I am the one who feels weary to the bone at the end of the day. That's when I know it's time to stop and get a refill.

Jesus needed time to be by Himself and be renewed in order go about God's work. He was moved with compassion for the lame, blind and the sick and He became weary. He knew when it was time to withdraw and so should I. Just as it took some effort to go out in the cold, so it takes a conscious effort to tap into a strength beyond myself. That strength is available, but I have to avail myself of it. When a gift is given to me, I have to stretch out my hands and receive it, hold it and unwrap it before it can become mine. So I have to receive God's strength, make it my own and use it as a gift. I need to listen to myself and know when it is time to stop, withdraw and be recharged.

6

The Answer is Yes

As surely as God is faithful,
our word to you has not been "Yes and No."
For the Son of God, Jesus Christ,
whom we proclaimed among you... was not
"Yes and No"; but in him it is always "Yes."
For in him every one of God's promises is a "Yes."
For this reason it is through him that we say
the "Amen," to the glory of God.
But it is God who establishes us with you
in Christ and has anointed us, by putting his seal
on us and giving us his Spirit
in our hearts as a first installment.
2 Corinthians 1:18-22

*I*n Him it is always "Yes." Jesus Christ was not "Yes and No," Paul says, but in Him it is always "Yes." Jesus Himself is the "yes" to us — He *says* yes to us and He *is* the yes, the positive answer to everything. Someone might say, "What is the question in the first place?" The question may be an existential one: "What is the meaning of my life? Why am I here, in this place and at this time in history?" It may be a question of "why?" when informed of a terminal illness or an untimely death. "Why me? Why now?"

The answer Jesus gives is "Yes." "In all that you go through, in all that happens to you, I am with you," Jesus says. Accepting that answer does not come without a struggle. Even John the Baptist, who was the forerunner of Christ, asked Jesus, *"Are you the one who is to come, or are we to wait for another?"* (Matt. 11:2-6). John the Baptist was not even sure of who Jesus was; perhaps John was too close to Jesus to see Him for who He was.

To us who are so far removed from all the events that Jesus used to establish Himself as the Son of God, Jesus says as he did to John:

"...the blind receive their sight, the lame walk,
the lepers are cleansed, the deaf hear,
the dead are raised, and
the poor have good news brought to them" (vs. 5).

What else did John need to convince him that Jesus was the Christ whose coming he had announced? What else do we need? Is it not enough? Jesus is the answer to people's needs.

Jesus still says "Yes" to us: "I am HE — look at what I am doing even today." Sure, we can always point to misery and death and destruction. Even in Jesus' days not everyone was healed, especially in places where there was unbelief. But Jesus says, "Look at what I have done and am still doing." Miracles still happen directly and indirectly through treatment and medication. Healing takes place through the Spirit which brings about reconciliation. When people face death there is a need to set one's house in order, especially in relationships. When it is possible to come together in a spirit of forgiveness and acceptance of each others' humanness, the Spirit is working. The Spirit of God, which was shown to the world by the being and doing of Jesus Christ, is still with us. Jesus still says "yes" to us and to the world. "I have overcome the world," He said, and that gives us the courage to say "yes" to life, in spite of what the future holds.

7
Prophetesses

By the rivers of Babylon —
there we sat down and there we wept
when we remembered Zion.
On the willows there we hung our harps....
How could we sing
the LORD's song in a foreign land?
Psalm 137:1-2,4

e are in a period of mourning, feeling acute pain. Sadness, anger and rage become part of us as more and more stories about abuse come to the surface. The silence is broken and the ugly truth is coming out. We are struck with unbelief when we hear that a trusted person is an abuser. It takes much courage to come out with the truth, and the support one hoped for may not be forthcoming. The victim's story may not be believed or accepted as having credibility. And if it is, each individual deals with it in a unique way, and this may not be understood.

I think of the tremendous strength we as women have when giving birth, when we are pushing to bring out the child — a new life. In the present time, enough energy is being generated through anger and indignation to bring forth a new reality. Women who have been and still are victims of abuse and inequality in every sphere of life are able to play a leading role in bringing this about. Women experience this issue from the heart and they are able to view abuse from the same perspective as those who have been victimized.

In Biblical times, prophets and prophetesses named the ugly truths, called for repentance and announced God's wrath. Huldah was one of those prophetesses whose advice was sought by King Josiah and his advisors. Huldah announced the damnation of Israel and the reason why and the verdict for Josiah, which was one of mercy. This spurred Josiah on to restoration rather than complacency (2 Kings 22:11-23:20).

We, as women, join in with other prophetesses by calling for a new approach where men and women and people of all classes and races are given equal rights. This new approach counters the destructiveness of hierarchal ordering of relationships as we see it in society and churches.

Prophets and prophetesses in the Bible spoke with an authority given to them by God and they called for justice and restoration. We too need to claim that authority and name injustices for what they are and use our energy to work for renewal. To do that, we first need to claim authority for ourselves as image-bearers of God. Huldah did not seem to have a problem with that authority even in a patriarchal society and her hearers accepted her verdict. Women in the role of prophetesses claim that God-given authority to speak out for themselves and for the victims of violence.

We sing a dirge for the brokenness of this world and we grieve intensely for the violence that is coming to the forefront with a new force. As prophetesses, we are not saying anything new; the Bible has always warned against injustice and the Old Testament is full of the writings of the prophets. I am thankful that women are finding their voice and are prepared to expose the truth. Others are angered enough to feel motivated to speak out for the oppressed — by protesting, by bearing the shame and the guilt, by calling for repentance and just relationships.

We need healing in all our roles and relationships in order to achieve wholeness. For men, this may mean relinquishing power, and for women, accepting and affirming themselves as image-bearers of God, redeemed by Jesus Christ.

We all have power — the power of choice. We have the power to effect good through the indwelling Spirit of God. Although the pain of abuse must be faced first on an individual basis, it may then become the catalyst for change in the public realm. We need to make personal decisions for change within ourselves and then together as a community. The prophets and prophetesses railed against injustice and domination, and God calls anew for people to do the same: to rise up in a protest born of pain. Women have suffered much indignity throughout the ages and that pain is now coming to light. But along with that pain is also coming a vision of a different, better way — a way that God is revealing with renewed insight and force. To relate in a new way is to respect one another as equals and as redeemed persons who are all called to be God's people in a hurting world. I for one will join the throng!

The Aroma of Christ

For we are the aroma of Christ to God
among those who are being saved
and among those who are perishing;
to the one a fragrance from death to death,
to the other a fragrance from life to life.
2 Corinthians 2:15-16

A chaplain is not always welcome. Sometimes I am seen as a representative of a system that is oppressive. Other times I am perceived as a grim reaper, a bearer of bad news. "Here is the chaplain, so it must be really serious," some people think. I see that reaction in the emergency room when the doctor gives bad news about the condition of a patient who was brought in by ambulance. The staff asks a chaplain to be present when the doctor breaks the news or when the family has to face a hopeless situation. A chaplain's visit is sometimes met with resistance, as with the patient who asked if I was a nun. Before I could explain that I was not, he told me to leave. He must have had some negative encounters with the sisters.

One patient in his sixties did not have long to live. He had a waxen look on his face and he was quite yellow. After I had introduced myself and we had talked for a while, he told me that he had quit going to church. His daughter was praying for him to surrender his life to

Christ. He said, "If God wants me, He should speak to me directly." I said that God was still speaking to him through His Word and through his daughter and others. We talked a few times and on the day that he heard that he was terminally ill with cancer, he told the nurse that he did not want me to visit him anymore, because to him that meant he was going to die.

Of course I did not feel very good about this turn of events. Where had I failed? Upon reflecting, I realized that for some, the good news of the gospel is indeed good news that gives strength and hope in a hopeless situation. However, for others, the call to faith in God is not perceived as good news, but rather something that is threatening and unsettling. I wondered what made this patient so resistant to God's invitation. Did he reject faith itself by not wanting to hear it, or were there people in his life who prevented him from accepting the gift of faith? Perhaps it was organized religion that turned him off. What did I represent for him?

I pondered over this failure to connect with him in a meaningful way. Perhaps my visits were meaningful and I did not know it. Should I have visited anyway or maybe written him a note? I respected his wish to be left alone, but I have not forgotten this man. I did pray for him that God would reach him where I could not, and I also knew that his daughter continued to pray for him.

Whatever it was, I have to believe that God knew what this patient needed. If it was the human expression of faith that caused him to resist accepting rest in God, I prayed that he would be lifted up beyond human failure to return to God's love. I prayed for grace for myself to let go and let God.

9
Land of Forgetfulness

Are your wonders known in the darkness,
or your saving help
in the land of forgetfulness?
Psalm 88:12

he patient I was asked to see was very depressed and only 21 years old. After we were introduced, there was silence and I asked her to tell me something about herself. She came from a broken home, but that was all she was willing to tell me. Her face showed immense pain. She then asked me to tell her the story of Lazarus and the rich man, which surprised me. I do not find that story very comforting, so I asked her what made her think of that part in the Bible. She said, "My mom says that there comes a time when God gives up and we will go to the land of forgetfulness." I wondered what she was saying to me. I asked, "Do you feel forgotten?" "Yes, I feel very lonely and God-forsaken." "How does it feel?" "Awful."

In order to better understand her, I thought back to the time when I was depressed and how communication with God was blocked. Black despair prevented me from experiencing any joy or feelings of thankfulness. And since I had so much to be thankful for and yet could not feel it, I then felt guilty.

Awful — that word expressed her feelings so well.

We talked some more and I told her that even when we do not feel God's presence, God is there and He will never leave us or forsake us even in our dark times. God's love can overcome the feeling of being forgotten and forsaken.

The Psalmist expresses a lament of abandonment in Psalm 88 and other psalms and these are given to us so that we may know we are not the only ones who at one time or another have suffered alienation from God. The next psalm, Psalm 89, expresses praise to God for God's steadfast love. What a change! The depressed person, I know, does not feel like praising God at all, but the darkness has to be experienced first before the light can shine through. So the girl and I prayed together for hope and grace and already she felt better because her loneliness had been broken by the presence of another person who understood. The pain of her loneliness was less intense now that it was shared. I prayed with her that her burden would become a little lighter and that someday soon she would feel some joy again. I also prayed that God would provide people to support her and give her professional help. I explained to her that God uses all these means to help us and that she would not have to carry the load by herself.

I did not see her again, and I find this the hard part of short-term counselling. I would have preferred to continue with her, but I had to trust that this one encounter was helpful and that she had been able to draw strength from it. I had to trust God for the rest and I had to commend her to God's care and trust that He had heard our prayer.

A Time for Grieving

Do not fear,
for I have redeemed you;
I have called you by name, you are mine.
Isaiah 43:1b

*J*n the last few weeks, there have been five stillbirths in our hospital. One of the most difficult tasks of the chaplains in our department is to minister to these parents in their time of need. Today was one of those days where I was with parents whose baby was born dead. Since the baby had been delivered by C-section, the mother had not seen the baby right away and she was now ready to view him before he would be taken away for burial.

After making arrangements with the morgue attendant, I went downstairs with the parents, the mother in a wheelchair. The baby had been washed and placed in a bassinet and the parents carefully moved closer, apprehensive at first and afraid of what they might see. It was amazing, however, that once they saw their child, they knew it was theirs and they took ownership. The baby was covered with a blanket, and only the little face was visible. The father removed the cover and together they looked at the face, the hands and the feet. They made some remarks how he resembled their other children and how tiny and sweet he looked. I said a prayer for this baby, commending him to God and giving him the name that the parents had chosen.

Back on the ward, the parents remarked that they were glad they had decided to go and see the baby. Time and again I have found it to be a very important step towards healing. Knowing what their child looked like was better than wondering about it, and from listening to patients who were never given the choice to view the baby, I know that recommending to see the baby is very helpful.

The parents had also requested that footprints be taken, and the morgue attendant and I managed to get a nice set of prints. A naming certificate was prepared and all together these mementoes became tangible reminders of this child; keepsakes that will become more precious as time goes on. Pictures of the baby were also provided by the hospital.

Our department has invested in acquiring booklets to give to parents whose babies have died and these speak to their experience so vividly that they find them very helpful. The readings help them understand their grief and that their reactions are shared with many. All in all, this pastoral involvement helps the parents deal with their grief. Initially, it is very frightening to go and view a deceased baby, but not one parent has regretted the decision to do so. A nurse told me that she had a stillborn baby a few decades ago and she regretted never having been given the choice to see or hold the baby. The decision that it would be too painful for her and her husband was made for them. They have been wondering ever since what the baby looked like.

It has become clear that giving the parents a choice

to see or not see the baby is giving them the power to choose. They are also encouraged to be in charge of funeral arrangements so that they may feel that they are in control. Sometimes parents want to hold a simple memorial service in the hospital chapel or in the funeral home. All these rituals provide a means of expressing grief for a child that was loved already before birth and will live on in the memory of the parents. On several occasions, I have held a very short service for a mother who regretted never having done anything for her child. A belated private ceremony has been one way for them to help ease the loss.

The text from Isaiah 43 was meant for the nation of Israel, but it is also very comforting for parents who believe that God loves them and their children. That's why giving the baby a name helps them to mourn their child as an individual who has a special place in their hearts and who is treasured as one of God's children.

11
Grief for a Baby

See, I have inscribed you on the
palms of my hands;
Isaiah 49:16

*T*he chapel was dimly lit, a single red rose graced the altar, a candle was burning and my short written meditation was ready. This was to be another memorial service for a full-term beautiful baby born dead. The parents were heart-broken and they had requested this service of remembrance. They needed to put words to their grief so that they could bring it to God prayerfully. These rituals are very healing, because it becomes a shared grief and it expresses in familiar and comforting words that which touches the mourners so deeply. They needed to do this in memory of their little son, whom they loved long before he was born.

Relatives of the young couple arrived, bringing flowers, and the nurse who brought the mom to the chapel stayed for the service as well. The couple's two-year old delighted in the burning candle and asked for the birthday cake. The innocence of little children brings smiles even in times of grief. The parents put some mementoes of the baby on the table: a picture, a lock of hair, a bracelet and a crib card. These are lovingly prepared by the nurses in Labour and Delivery for the parents to take home. All of these are treasured, tangible things that have proven to be very comforting when grief is acute, but also later as a precious memory.

The memorial service was short. We sang a favourite song of the grandmother and a song that was sung at the couple's wedding. This brought tears to the eyes of the grandfather. Who knows what memories he had of his daughter; I realized how little we know of people's life stories. The meditation brought sober reality into the context of God's love and grace at this time of grieving. This baby had been baptized shortly after he was lifted from the womb and I presented a candle to the parents as a keepsake.

I was again struck by how healing these simple gestures were and how this being together comforted the parents and family. After the service, we listened to the tape by Carey Landry: "Lay your hands, gently lay your hands." I thought, "Yes, Lord, lay your hands gently on all of us."

12

Mother's Day

Therefore I am content with weaknesses
for whenever I am weak, then I am strong.
2 Corinthians 12:10

*K*aren was a long-term psychiatric patient. She is the victim of horrible abuse by her father. Karen completely blocked out these abusive episodes by assuming personalities other than her own. Karen had five such personalities and they all took turns presenting themselves depending on the situation. One personality repeatedly told Karen that she was no good and that she had no right to live. Many attempts at suicide were the result of this voice talking to her. Karen is working with a psychiatrist to integrate these personalities and to overcome this Dissociative Identity Disorder and she has needed to be hospitalized for weeks on end.

For some time, Karen managed to function fairly well with the help of weekly visits to the psychiatrist. But at a certain point in her adult life, flashbacks of the childhood abuse began and Karen became seriously disturbed. One night I came through our emergency department and there she was. A tube in her nose drained black fluid from her stomach. She had overdosed again and her stomach was being pumped.

Mother's Day had set off a whole series of feelings

that became too overwhelming for her. Karen felt very guilty about the sexual abuse, as if she were to blame. Karen said that she loved her father despite what he did to her, but she felt anger towards her mother, for pretending not to know what was going on and for never interfering. This realization is very hard to face for victims of abuse. Mother's Day was not a happy day for Karen in a society where motherhood is portrayed as gloriously perfect. For Karen, the ideal and reality were too far removed from each other.

The next day when I visited Karen on the ward, she said, "I was so glad to see you last night; it was like seeing an angel. I wanted to hug you, but I was so grimy." She then asked, "Does God still love me?" I did not know of her need for a hug and what that would have meant to her. If I had known and responded, she would have felt the reaffirmation of God's love which she needed so much. There was a tremendous amount of guilt after this suicide attempt and she needed to feel forgiveness in a tangible way. At times it is hard to know how far to go in my reassurance of the suffering. Karen has come a long way towards healing and we thank God for it together. I continue to trust God to guide my expression of pastoral care. Even if I fail to be tuned in to a patient's need, God is able to use my efforts for good. That relieves me of needing to be perfect and it allows the Spirit of God to do the work in her. After all, it is God who works in people's hearts and I can only be thankful to play a very small part in it.

13
Flowers

As for mortals, their days are like grass;
they flourish like a flower of the field;
for the wind passes over it, and it is gone,
and its place knows it no more.
But the steadfast love of the LORD is
from everlasting to everlasting
on those who fear him.
Psalm 103:15-17

*O*ne of the advantages of visiting the sick in the hospital is having an opportunity to enjoy flowers. Many patients receive so many flowers that they are lined up on the floor, some have a vase of homegrown flowers from the garden, while others have no flowers at all.

When I enter a room, I take note of the flowers as an indication of the patient's support system or the lack thereof. Cards, a tiny Christmas tree or posters at the bedside are tokens of love brought into the hospital. When loved ones are far away they have flowers sent to the patient. One elderly patient had a bouquet in her room that was sent to her by her daughter. Since the patient was bedridden, the flowers were not taken care of and a faded remnant of the once glorious bouquet stood there for weeks.

When I see that happen, I realize how important it is to have someone there to tend to flowers and plants and to the patient. Without that care, the flowers become a sign of abandonment. Sending flowers without being able to be there for the patient is only second best. That cannot always be avoided and then the human touch will have to be provided by someone else. It may be a volunteer or a friend. A chaplain can be a welcome guest in the lonely lives of the elderly. A chaplain is able to bring comfort by listening to and reminiscing with the patient. I have heard pioneer stories to last a lifetime, and many tales of being taken away from home in Poland or Russia to Siberia. There is a depth of wisdom in their reflecting and these stories are usually not told in bitterness. There was always something good in a bad situation. One woman remembered the beautiful flowers in Siberia. Flowers bring cheer and beauty. The saying, "Say it with flowers," is only true up to a point; we also have to express our love through words and deeds.

Faded flowers are a reminder of how fleeting our lives are, and this text in Psalm 103 came to mind when I saw that dried-up bouquet. I shared these thoughts with this elderly woman and she agreed that the steadfast love of God never fades and never ends. I was glad we could together reflect on the never-ending love of God, who comforts us *as a mother comforts her child* (Isa. 66:13). Loneliness is a hallmark of the elderly but those who know the Lord may enjoy the comfort about which Isaiah wrote.

14

The Everlasting Arms

The eternal God is your refuge,
and underneath are the everlasting arms.
Deuteronomy 33:27a (NIV)

*O*n this day before Christmas, I had just finished looking after the needs of a family whose
93-year old mother had passed away when my
beeper went off. It was a s.t.a.t. call from emergency. As
I went down on the elevator, I thought, "Please not
another death. It's Christmas tomorrow and we still
have a Christmas service to take care of." When I came
to the desk, I was asked to be with the parents of a one-
month old baby who had been found limp and unrespon-
sive in his crib. Doctors tried to revive him to no avail
and the parents were told that he was dead.

The shock and grief in cases of crib death or sudden
infant death syndrome are indescribable. The father
said he could never enjoy Christmas again. The mother
was too stricken with grief to say anything. I took both
of them into the trauma room to say their final goodbyes to the baby. Mother Irene held her baby, stroked
and kissed him, covering him with tears. There is nothing as sad as a dead baby. I sat with Irene, because the
father had stormed out of the room saying he could not
stand this any longer. As we waited for the coroner to
come, I tried to say something comforting. And what is

there to say? They had no faith in God, no church connection, no pastor or priest to call.

When the coroner finally came and finished his questions, Irene was ready to hand the baby over. But instead of putting him back on the stretcher, she gave the baby to me. Somehow she could not bear to put him on that cold bed, so she entrusted her baby to my arms. The human touch was very much needed in this utterly sad moment. I gently put the baby back on the bed and blessed him. The parents left the hospital broken-hearted and I told them they could call me if they needed help or support.

My heart was heavy as I returned to the office, needing to be by myself for a while. As I reflected on this sad event, I thought about Irene's gesture of handing me the baby. I felt I had been on holy ground. Those arms had represented to her love and compassion. Somehow love had been communicated and Irene had reached out for consolation. If I could convey a message of love by just being there in her pain, *how much more will [our] Father in heaven give good things to those who ask Him* (Matt. 7:11). How much more compassion does God show than we ever can!

That afternoon I gave the Christmas message in the chapel. As I spoke, I felt I had gained a new understanding of how wide and deep God's love must be to have sent Jesus Christ into the world to become one of us and experience grief. Jesus knew what suffering was and what utter desolation felt like. And His arms are stretched out to receive our grief, along with that of Irene and her husband. We too may give our loved ones over to the everlasting arms who take better care of them than we can. I thank God that somehow through my presence, a message of love was conveyed, and I pray that this couple will be comforted in their grief and experience more of this love as they continue on their life's journey.

15

Home

For we know that if the earthly tent
we live in is destroyed,
we have a building from God,
a house not made with hands,
eternal in the heavens.
2 Corinthians 5:1

A visit with a truckdriver who needed surgery to correct an old injury made me reflect on the meaning of home. Home means so many things. We have a home on earth: our body. Paul says in 1 Corinthians that when this tent we live in, our body here on earth, is torn down, God will have a house in heaven for us to live in, a home He Himself has made which will last forever.

The truckdriver told me that his truck was his home; the cabin had all the modern conveniences he needed, such as a TV and microwave oven. He loved being on the highway, enjoying the sights. Marriages had broken up because of his long absences from home, he said, but he was free, although, he added regretfully, he did miss his children. So he paid a price for his freedom. He did not accept the responsibility of raising his children because travelling the highways was in his blood. As he continued to reflect on his life, he said that he was actually doing the same thing to his children that his father had done to him. His father had abandoned his family when the children were young. So the security of a home base had never been a part of his life and this obviously still affected him, seeing the desire he had to be on the road all the time. What was he running away from, I wondered.

A good home means a safe place to come home to. There are so many expressions that convey this message — homey, homely, homecoming, homemade, homemaker. All these words have to do with a place that people have made into a community where they eat, sleep and talk together, and where joys and sorrows are shared. It is a physical place that holds many familiar things, heirlooms however simple. Houses have certain smells and sounds and views, but it is the people who make it a home.

Patients in the hospital always talk about going home, and when the day actually comes, there is rejoicing. When I am tired of a day's work, I cannot think of anything I'd like to do better than to go home and relax, eat and drink, light a candle and feel safe. It is best, of course, when someone is there to greet me and be there with me. I thank God that there has always been a home for me. When I go back to my native Holland, I am reminded of the good and bad times and of the love with which I was surrounded. I grieve for the homeless, here in Canada and in those countries where there is so much displacement and homelessness. But even there, people make a little corner for themselves, if only from cardboard, which they call home.

When Adam and Eve were sent out of their first home, it must have been a terrifying experience. Yet God has always remained our home, our dwelling place. Here on earth, we long for a homecoming and, as Paul says, God has prepared that place for us. When I see the elderly and how their bodies do not function as they used to, I realize that their earthly home is decaying. I rejoice in knowing that for them and less imminent for my own body, it does not end there. Jesus said that He went to prepare a place for us (John 14:2). I am sure that that home will provide all we long for: rest, beauty, love, joy and communion with others in perfect harmony.

The truckdriver is roaming the highways and it gives him satisfaction. The day will come when he will not be able to drive his truck around anymore and he will look for a place to settle. But he will not have any roots and permanent relationships. He will miss something and, as I suggested to him, he could give some thought to the eternal home, where he will always be welcome.

16
Living Letters

And you show that you are a letter of Christ,
prepared by us, written not with ink
but with the Spirit of the living God,
not on tablets of stone
but on tablets of human hearts.
2 Corinthians 3:3

To the writing of letters there is no end. Letter-writing is an important part of my life, and receiving personal letters is a joy that I would not want to miss. Letters have helped me stay in touch with loved ones and lifted me up in hard times.

My letter-writing started already when Job, my husband, left for Canada shortly after our engagement. A period of two years and three months of letter-writing gave us an opportunity to put our thoughts and feelings onto paper, besides giving accounts of what was happening in our lives. Plans for Job's return to Holland and for our wedding were discussed and these letters were the lifeline in our relationship. There was always the expectation and anticipation in waiting for these letters during those years. After our wedding and departure from Holland, the letter-writing continued, now from daughter to parents and vice versa. This weekly ritual sustained the love bond and family ties. Many letters have crossed the ocean — up to this day close to 5,000 have been sent off and received.

In the early years of our marriage, these letters from home kept me going and they were again an important link in a relationship that meant so much. Our family grew up and busy years followed, but the letters were always there as an important presence. They announced visits and conveyed best wishes for all kinds of occasions.

When our oldest daughter, Nelly, went to college, married and moved away, another phase of letter-writing started. The weekly ritual consisted of writing two letters minimum and often more to brothers, sisters and friends. Letters are great to write and great to receive. The faithfulness on both sides shows a commitment to the relationship and a caring beyond words. It shows who we are.

So it is with the lives of Christians: We are letters of Christ. We don't even have to say much, but what or how we say it makes a difference. How we live, how we spend our time and energy, and how we conduct ourselves is a testimony of what the Spirit of God has written on our hearts. Knowing that we are loved, we are able to love in return. What lives inside of us is shown in our attitudes and lifestyles.

In biblical times, letters of recommendation were often mentioned. They served to tell the recipient of the letter that a particular person was suitable for the position they were recommended for. Paul, for instance, in Romans 16:1 commends Phoebe, a deaconess, to the Church in Rome in a letter of recommendation. These letters were highly valued. These letters were of a different nature than the personal ones. However, Paul did not only write letters of recommendation; he also shared of his personal experiences in prison, for instance. Letters in whatever form, convey a message from one person to another. Letters can, of course, also bring bad news or be a means of expressing negative messages.

God's letter to us as believers is not a negative message because it contains the promise of life. And if it is received in the same spirit in which it was written — a spirit of love and compassion for the people of God — then it becomes a precious possession. God's letters can be read over and over again, studied and applied to our own situation. When patients in the hospital receive letters and greeting cards, they keep them close in order to enjoy them as reminders of the care the sender has shown. The card industry has developed many beautiful verses for cards, but an added written note makes it so much more personal. God's letter is a personal note to all of us, inviting us to read it, enjoy it and draw strength from it in whatever circumstance.

I have saved letters from my late father as a reminder of who he was. I will do the same with my mother's letters. The thoughts and love expressed by all the letters and cards received over the years have become part of me. The spirit of God's letter is the basis for all of these relationships. The spirit of the letter from God is read and absorbed by us as followers of Christ. It makes us who we are: walking testimonies of the grace that is revealed to us in a "letter," through which we become living letters ourselves.

17

Hope Returns

Therefore be serious and discipline yourselves
for the sake of your prayers.
1 Peter 4:7b

ometimes we are not able to pray; it simply does not work. This was the case for Susan, a very depressed patient who asked for some help in getting back in touch with God. But how? Her mind was not alert, but confused and in turmoil. Susan suffered from severe depression repeatedly, and hopelessness was very much a part of her frame of mind when I visited. "Why did God do this to me? Why can I not be healed and look after my children?" she asked. To add insult to injury, the father of her children was planning to take them to live elsewhere, because Susan was not able to look after them. What grief!

Sometimes I feel dumfounded by the complexity of problems people face. I don't know what to say in the face of such defeat. I can only ask God to help me find the right approach. I knew I must not say anything that would not make sense to her, that she could not "hear" because of her pain; her mind would not absorb it and she would be no better off. What to do or say?

Drawing on the experiences of other involvements with depressed patients, I turned to the Scriptures and let the Word do its work. These words of wisdom and comfort in Lamentations 3:19-24, for instance, were better than mine:

> *The thought of my affliction and my homelessness*
> *is wormwood and gall!*
> *My soul continually thinks of it*
> *and is bowed down within me.*
> *But this I call to mind, and therefore I have hope:*
> *The steadfast love of the* LORD *never ceases,*
> *His mercies never come to an end;*
> *They are new every morning;*
> *great is your faithfulness.*
> *"The* LORD *is my portion," says my soul,*
> *"therefore I will hope in Him."*

Somehow this reading did something, because it spoke to her depressed spirit, it acknowledged the feelings and did not shy away from the pain. And hope did return because here was something solid to hang onto: the Lord's unfailing love! This passage helped Susan because it spoke of her pain — yes, it was real. The approach of "trust in God and all will be well" is not what depressed people want to hear. They need to hear that their pain and despair are genuine and that God knows about it. They are reaching out for hope, for something to get them through.

It is difficult for someone who has not learned to trust in God to start doing this in a state of depression. For some, God is a miracle worker, who fails them when things go wrong. I talked with Susan, struggling with her to understand that God does not take the pain away, but He can make something good and beautiful out of every situation. And God provides help in the form of medical intervention and therapy to find healing for the after-effects of abuse if that is needed. God also provides people to be there and give support. Susan, however, did not feel that she had any friends who understood her. Her withdrawal from others around her closed the door for communication and for the sharing of pain. We prayed that she could again be open to the support of others and we prayed that God would provide the right person for her. Susan, in the midst of her despair, found it hard to believe that God was weaving the tapestry of her life, using the dark threads of her depression to bring beauty.

As we talked, we tried to reflect on signs of God's love and mercy. Even the fact that her children were now cared for by someone else could be seen as a good thing because Susan herself certainly was not able to do justice to her role as parent. Together we prayed for strength, for a glimmer of hope and for a time when she could again look after her children. Hope did return, slowly, after many sessions. Others may not be so fortunate. I do not know the answer to that, but I can hang on with them and for them, praying that some day God's love and mercy will be completed in those devastated lives as well.

18

Morning by Morning New Mercies I See

*...when I think of you on my bed, and
meditate on you in the watches of the night;*
Psalm 63:6

*O*ne of the tasks of a chaplain in the Pastoral Care Department of the Catholic hospital where I worked is to bring a meditation or prayer via the intercom in the mornings and evenings. This was started by the founders of the hospital and it has become a tradition that is much appreciated by patients and staff alike. The chaplains adapt this message to the time of year, such as Advent, Lent, summer, winter, spring or Thanksgiving. Often patients and staff comment on the message because it speaks to them in a special way. On the 5th of May, I read the poem "Poppies in Flander's Field." Many people commented on it because of all the memories it sparked among the Dutch and Canadian people. Sometimes people phone or come into the department and ask for a copy of the readings. Our director sometimes improvises a prayer and often she adds, "Do not forget that random act of kindness."

In our meditations, we may remind our staff and patients to look beyond the losses and changes in health-care and view them as challenges and opportunities for new openings. Long-term patients especially, wait at night for the prayer to come through, and some even position themselves by the door so that they will hear it more clearly. In the morning, the sound often gets lost in the hustle and bustle of the hospital, but at night it is more quiet; the visitors are gone and patients are ready to retire. A patient may ask when I visit, "Was it you who said the prayer last night? I really liked it." Many can relate to the spiritual focus of our hospital and, because they are very vulnerable, they are more open to the meaning of these readings. A verse that may not strike a healthy person as having a special meaning may have an impact on a sick person. Patients may be facing an operation or waiting restlessly for the results of a test to come back, and the pressure is strong. A word of encouragement is just what is needed at those times.

I was with a couple and their parents in a time of deep sorrow, and that evening I chose the meditation entitled "The Weaver," and they felt it was especially for them. God, as the weaver, weaves in sorrow, but, it goes on to say, the dark threads are as needed in the weaver's skillful hands as the threads of gold and silver are in the pattern that God has planned.

Hospitalization makes people vulnerable; they are often fearful and apprehensive about what is going to happen. Chaplains are not able to visit everyone nor always be there in their neediest times. Our staff calls for pastoral care when there is a need, but some are still missed. Therefore, the morning and evening meditations fill a need for spiritual comfort, encouragement and hope, and they serve as a reminder that God never leaves nor forsakes us.

19
Binder of Wounds

*[God] heals the brokenhearted and
binds up their wounds.*
Psalm 147:3

I gave this meditation to chaplains and
spouses at a retreat in Grand Rapids in
June of 1994.
This morning I would like to tell you a little bit about my
faith life, and I am sure many of you can relate to what
I am going to say. At the beginning of my training and
work as a chaplain, I enjoyed a closeness with God that
kept me going and that gave me the energy to do much
hard work. Since last year however, I have felt like I am
just plodding along; my energy level is low and I often
feel depressed. There are many factors that contribute to
this, of course. First of all, in Alberta, there is a major
upheaval in health care right now, and the hospital
where I work will close as an active treatment hospital
and be changed into a community health centre.
Catholic health care is really on the block. We don't
know how this will affect our positions as chaplains, but
there will be major changes and much adapting to do if
the pastoral care department is to be maintained.

Then there is the endless debate in the Christian
Reformed Church about women in office. Everyone is
getting tired of it, and the endless arguments about

women without even giving women a vote in this matter is extremely discouraging and grievous for those of us who feel called to the ministry. I feel that grace and redemption are completely left out of the picture.

My husband's brother, Morris, died of a brain tumor last summer, not even a year ago. He was only fifty eight; I knew this brother from the years that we went to school together. When he was first diagnosed, the family rallied together in prayer. Many groups were set in motion to pray; he set his house in order, asked for forgiveness of those he felt needed to forgive him and the perfect setting was there for God to bring healing. We hoped, yet nine months later we stood around his grave, on a beautiful summer day. Death seemed so unreal. A man who meant so much to his family and to his faith community was no more with us.

Before Christmas, the pastoral care department held chapel services for the Advent season. I gave a meditation on the theme of "JOY." I talked about the joy of the angels, of Mary and Elizabeth, whose baby leapt in her womb, and of the shepherds. A nice service all in all. When the patients filed out, they shook my hand, but one elderly lady, leaning on her cane, tapped me on the shoulder and said, "Sister, how about the children in Sarajevo?" I said, "We can only do the best we can, where God places us." I did not mean it however, as I had the same question: What about those children? That's the question of suffering, of course. I talk a lot with adult survivors of sexual and ritual abuse, in the hospital and in support groups, I see their wrecked lives, and I hear the same question. As one patient put it: "It is not only that I suffered abuse way back, but I relive it over and over again. Will it ever stop?" The victims of abuse carry the after-effects in their bodies and spirits. One survivor asked, "Where was God when abuse took place and how come that healing of memories is too hard to obtain?" The memories and flashbacks occur whether the person wants it or not. I hurt with these people. I am having a difficult time with the images of God; it would be so nice to feel close to the God of Psalm 23, which I have read so many times at the bedsides of others. The image of God as the "Good Shepherd" has comforted many, many people. I am praying to get that comfortable feeling back myself of Jesus who, with outstretched hands, says, *"Come to me, all you that are weary and are carrying heavy burdens, and I will give you rest"* (Matt. 11:28). I cannot find rest, not yet. I am experiencing loss, by the aging of parents, by the aging of our own bodies, by the suffering in the world, by having seen too many unanswered prayers, by having seen so much death. I was with a young mom who was bubbling over with joy at the birth of a healthy baby boy. She said, "God is so good!" But I knew that next door was a new mom who was tearfully struggling to accept that her baby had Down's Syndrome. Is God really so good, I wondered.

In my searching, I found an image of God that helped me and is still helping me: that of the "Binder of Wounds." We find this image in Ezekiel 34:16: *"I will... bind up the injured, and I will strengthen the weak....";* and in Hosea 6:1: *"Come, let us return to the LORD; for it is He who has torn, and He will heal us; He has struck down, and He will bind us up."* In Job 5:18, it says, *"For [God] wounds, but He binds up; He strikes but His hands heal."*

The image of God whose hands are healing became very meaningful when I was at another retreat. I find it amazing that when we really prayerfully search for answers, we do hear or read or come to understand in some way what God is saying in answer to our need. At this retreat, slides were shown of the prodigal son painted by Rembrandt, the Dutch painter. I love those paintings! Rembrandt lived from 1606-1669. This Dutch painter lost two wives and four children in his lifetime, so he knew what grief was. The retreat leader asked us to pay attention to the hands of the father embracing the son who was kneeling in front of him, having just returned from his journey. And this is what touched me deeply: the hands were different. One was a slender female hand and the other was a short, stubby male hand. This was in the 17th century! I am not sure if Rembrandt purposely painted those hands the way he did, or if it just turned out that way, but those hands came to have a prophetic meaning. That's how Rembrandt saw the father who imaged God.

Going back to the text in Job, I made the connection: For God wounds but He also binds up; God injures, but His hands also heal. I think of those hands, one a man's and one a woman's, and that comforts me. And I know that this too was a necessary stage in my life in order to help me really be with other people; not to simply come with ready answers, but to struggle and search with them for meaning.

Slowly, I am learning, but also still searching. Does God wound and injure? It is sometimes difficult to reconcile an omnipotent and all-powerful God with a compassionate God. Why does God not intervene more in the suffering of humanity? Does God not want to or is God unable to intervene? Questions like these often just confuse. It is helpful, therefore, to put the emphasis on a loving God whose heart was broken over the people of Israel, who were often punished for their waywardness, but who were also restored and healed again. God's everlasting faithfulness, HESED, has always been there and still is and always will be. God is a God who embraces humanity with both hands — tender hands and strong hands. God's love is so far and deep and wide that even where He sees the ravages of sin, He does not withdraw or take distance in times of difficulty. God is right here, embracing us with those hands, and in the end, love will prevail.

Therefore, I can now say that into God's hands, the tender one and the strong one, I commend my life, my spirit, my loved ones, my future, my searching and my joys. And maybe, looking back, this answer that I gave to the wise old woman was not so bad after all. We can only do the best we can where we are. But then there are these hands that are holding us, comforting us when we need it, but also lifting us up from our knees to be binders of wounds ourselves, questions and all. And that is very life-giving and empowering for us as chaplains and for all of us.

An Anniversary

I will sing of your steadfast love,
O LORD, forever;
with my mouth I will proclaim
your faithfulness to all generations.
Psalm 89:1

*O*ur 40th wedding anniversary was the occasion for all of our children and grandchildren to be with us to celebrate. We spent as much time together as was possible for two weeks and we walked, talked, and sang songs around the open fire like we did on family camping trips many years ago.

We held an open house for family and friends and it was an intense time of making the most of whatever time we had available. We reminisced about the time when Job and I first came to Canada and I remembered my first birthday in Canada on the train trip from Halifax to Edmonton in 1955. We remembered our camping holidays and many other things. Our children tried as many of the Dutch sayings and songs as they knew how.

Our hearts were filled with thankfulness to God for blessing our family in this way. We have fifteen grandchildren who have been baptized and who are now learning to walk in the light of God's face (Ps. 89:15). Even the little ones who cannot even talk yet, know when it is time to be quiet and as we see them fold their little hands to pray we are amazed. We often marvel at how God has blessed our efforts of raising our children and that in spite of our failures, God has been faithful. I can say one thing that, though we were not always right or wise, Job and I were sincere in our love for the children and in our commitment to our Creator and Redeemer.

We started out very young and inexperienced as far as parenting was concerned and we went by common sense and by what we had learned in our families of origin. And somehow, the four of them have become responsible and hard-working adults, devoted partners and parents, sincere in their faith commitment. It is humbling that the grace of God has become evident in spite of our sometimes damaging approach to the shaping of their personalities. We are convinced that God honoured our commitment to the task before us and that He worked His purposes through us as children of grace. As long as we realize our dependence on God and are ready to admit that no matter how hard we try we are only human, God will do the rest. We bring to our lives the hurts and blessings from our past and our upbringing and we can only do the best we know how. If everything were perfect, we would not have to struggle and our characters would not be developed the way they are. We watched our children develop through their own learning experiences, some of which we wish they did not have to go through. Yet these shaped them into who they are today, because they were always surrounded by God's love and our love.

On the last day of our vacation in Jasper, a mountain resort, a magnificent rainbow displayed its splendor against the dark sky and against the mountains after a rainshower. Its colours were bright and formed a perfect arc from beginning to end. It came at a time when we were filled with thankfulness and it was a profound reminder of God's covenant with children and children's children. It spoke of the One who remains faithful to all generations of those who fear Him, and who will not remove from them His steadfast love.

──── 21 ────
A Renewed Focus

Trust in the LORD with all your heart,
and do not rely on your own insight.
In all your ways acknowledge him and he
will make straight your paths.
Proverbs 3:5-6

*W*e had a busy summer in 1995, with all our children present for our 40th wedding anniversary. After all the visiting was over, we returned to our quiet lifestyle. We cleaned up the aftermath of the time that our home was a guesthouse. A stack of cards reminded us of a happy time, and the plants we have far outlived the flower arrangements that were given to us. We said our tearful goodbyes again and then picked up our lives with the pictures and the memories of a family get-together that none of us will ever forget.

My work as a chaplain is another part of my life, a commitment to which God called me later in life. When I think about it, I realize that my life has been full and still is. Now that this stage of my ministry in an acute care centre is coming to an end, I am entering a time of transition. The changes in health care institutions are a result of massive cutbacks in government funding. No high risk or major surgeries will be done anymore in three out of the five hospitals in Edmonton, Alberta.

This change asks for a refocusing of pastoral care. One of our tasks is to be of support to staff, who are either receiving lay-off notices or facing increased workloads. These changes affect patient care in a negative way and there is increased anxiety all over. Some surgeons refuse to be part of a health care system where there is not sufficient back-up of intensive care when complications arise from surgery or in cases of serious accidents. These surgeons look elsewhere to do their work. Nurses are pressed for time and cannot give adequate care nor the personal attention to patients that they would like to give.

Bedside ministry is not the same anymore for chaplains in community health centres, since they are not called as often for deaths and trauma cases. All in all, I am facing the end of this stage of my ministry and, come fall, I will take my leave from the hospital at which I have worked for seven years — seven years spent with the sick, dying, grieving and depressed, but years that were good nevertheless. This work has come to a natural ending. I do not know what comes next, because I am asking God to show me the way. I am not retiring from service, but in what way, shape or form this service will continue, I am not yet sure. So travel with me, open to the marvel of God's leading. I do not believe that God has led me this far to sit back and rest — not yet. I trust that there is still a task for me. Maybe not an official one, but I am sure one of encouragement and a spurring on to accept the grace of God as partners of Christ (Heb. 3:14).

22

A New Assignment

In returning and rest you shall be saved;
in quietness and in trust shall be your strength.
Isaiah 30:15b

After our vacation, I entered a new stage in my ministry as a chaplain. I began working in a half-time position in another health centre with the same assignment as before in Obstetrics, Labour and Delivery, Surgery and all areas of the hospital when on call. I am grateful for this new opportunity; I work twenty hours a week so I have more time to be at home without feeling too tired to do anything else but the routine things.

A recent decision in Church life, however, showed again that mutuality in relationships and in ministry is not practiced in our community of faith. Freedom in Christ calls for open arms to receive with gladness and joy the giftedness of men and women, so that each may feel supported and loved in their chosen area of work. That would release the tremendous potential for outreach because then there would be a free flow of the power of God. Instead, there is fear, suspicion and distrust of women entering the office of elder and minister. Internal strife prevents the Church from being the healing presence it could be, and as long as it keeps on turning on its own axle instead of forming ever-widening circles, the Church will lose its effectiveness.

Therefore, I need to take distance from this troubled situation until such a time that women are better received and welcomed. A temporary reprieve hopefully, but a necessary one for the centering and reclaiming of who I am. Hopefully, I will gain a new perspective.

When I first started out on the path to the chaplaincy, I once asked God how I could change the Church. I am sure God smiled at my arrogance and these words were clearly imprinted on my mind: "Leave it to me, it is my work." When the need for change becomes my agenda, I am in trouble. That change may happen in a totally different way than I expect. For now, I focus on my work in this community health centre and getting acquainted in a new environment. I also must continue to be in close relationship with God in order to discern where God wishes me to be and where He can use me.

I need time to process all the changes, though. I will continue to minister in the hospital and be available wherever I am needed. Frustrations elsewhere, however, distract from the inner peace that I need in order to be with the sick and dying. Others will carry the load in places where God calls them and I will go about my ministry. Lord, keep me from bitterness and help me to focus on your gifts in others and in myself.

23
Reconnecting

For I [Paul] am longing to see you
[the believers in Rome] so that I may share
with you some spiritual gift to strengthen you —
or rather so that we may be
mutually encouraged by each others' faith,
both yours and mine.
Romans 1:11-12

*M*utual encouragement — how much we need it! Those of us in special ministries need to continually be uplifted by believers because this is not a road to be travelled alone. We just came back from a restful holiday, although I found it hard to relax. Returning to our home base and connecting again with the people we know so well felt good. I realized again how I miss the company of people with whom we communicate.

Since a chaplain always gives of him or herself and is with people as a supporter and encourager, I often feel drained and in need of rest. The quiet presence of my husband is healing, but I need encouragement from others as well. In my need to take distance from being involved with crisis and grief situations, I sometimes make the mistake of not spending time with God's Word. I know that Word is engrained in my being, but I also need to feed that faith daily, and when I use the Scriptures only for reading to others and not for my own nurture, I am short-changing myself.

Coming home, therefore, and settling into the routine was good. The demands of life are also there with a renewed urgency, but with self-discipline, I can make a new commitment to spend time with God. If the giving of self is not balanced by receiving, the source runs dry and ministry loses its effectiveness. The encouragement of others is so needed and the few times that a patient offered to pray for me were a gift that was gratefully accepted. It made the load somewhat lighter. Therefore, I was pleasantly surprised when believers from another congregation became my prayer partners. When I ask for prayer, I do not ask for attention, but rather for strength to go on.

The apostle Paul longed to be with the believers in Rome for mutual support and to hear them share their faith that was severely tested in those times. In our time, faith in God is being tested in different ways and we do come in contact with dark forces. As chaplains, we are faced with many issues that are not addressed in the Bible, such as organ transplants, prolonging of life, termination of life, etc. Therefore, we need to be continually open to the Spirit of God to guide us in the application of His Word in practical ways.

The faith community should always be prayerfully engaged in lifting up those in special ministries, praying for the power of God to be released in them. It cannot be done alone.

24
Facing the Truth

But speaking the truth in love,
we must grow up in every way into him
who is the head, into Christ....
Ephesians 4:15

J met him in the waiting room. He told me
that his wife was in the operating room
having some device put in whereby the pain
medication could be administered more evenly and reg-
ularly than before. When I told him who I was, it was
clear that he was glad to have someone to talk to. "It"
was diagnosed only a few months ago, he said, and his
wife was going for treatments which were making her
very sick. He confided that it was all so hard to take
because she was only in her forties. The children had
their own lives to live and he felt quite alone in sup-
porting his wife. He spent much time waiting in hospitals while she was undergoing her treatments and tests.

Mr. Hope talked of going back and forth between
hoping for a cure or a remission and accepting reality.
The doctors were not promising anything, but you never
know! Hope kept this couple going and they also knew of
the hope of eternal life and that made communicating
much easier. I noted that in this conversation, he never
mentioned the word cancer, although we both knew that
this was the disease we were talking about. Shock,

denial and acceptance are all part of the grieving process, and not being able to say the word cancer is part of the denial and struggle for acceptance. Patients and family members each struggle in their own way to sort out their feelings of fear, anger, hope, despair and so much more. While people are sorting out all these feelings, they often cannot bring themselves to mention the disease by name, because of all the suffering and indignities it implies. There is fear of dying, and concern for the spouse or other loved ones who will eventually have to carry on without the patient. Somehow it is easier to talk about a heart attack than about cancer.

Another series of visits which I made many years ago came to mind. I called on a patient who was causing problems for the staff because of her mistrust and negative attitude. This patient had suffered serious injuries and faced many surgeries and a long period of rehabilitation. As we talked, she would say things like, "Before *it* happened..." or "Since *it* happened..." I did not probe or ask questions and it was only after many visits that she started to trust me enough to let me ask her if she cared to tell me what "it" was and what had happened. It was only then that she told me her story, and from then on our talks were more open. The secret "it" was out in the open and we both knew what we were talking about.

When the diagnosis of cancer is given, it takes time to sink in and be processed. Some people talk openly about it and some do not and this simply cannot be forced. I am uncomfortable when family members wish to keep the diagnosis from the patient, even though it's out of concern for him or her. I find that doing that only makes for a lack of openness in relationships. The reverse can also happen when the patient does not want her loved ones to know or one particular person is not informed of the truth. One patient did not want her husband, who was elsewhere, to know how seriously ill she was. Only after her death was he informed, and this only deprived him of the opportunity to say good-bye and bring closure to their life together. Sometimes I have an opportunity to talk about this secrecy with patients or family members by asking how they themselves would feel if the truth was kept from them. This makes them think, but the decision is still up to them what to do with it.

In all these situations, we should not forget that support can only be received when we feel free to share our problems, fears and struggles. If we keep others in the dark, we also keep them from praying for us and helping us in our pain. We all need to remind ourselves of that once in a while. I often think of the man in the waiting room, who was willing to let me be part of his struggles and, by putting his thoughts into words, may have come a bit closer to accepting and living with that dreaded disease — cancer.

25
Friendship

Better is a neighbour who is nearby
than kindred who are far away.
Proverbs 27:10b

*W*hat is friendship? It is having someone with whom to share. It is not so much *doing* things for each other, as *being* there for each other. Friendship means being available for each other when there is a need to cry or a need to share a joy or achievement. When burdened by a family concern, it is a blessing to have someone who understands, who does not correct or preach or give advice. Real listening means hearing the other out without giving in to the urge to interject or interrupt. Real listening means asking for clarification to check if we are still on track and it means giving feedback.

In a troubled situation, we may not be reasonable or loving in what we are saying, but we need to be allowed to express ourselves strongly at times to let off steam, without our friend saying, "You should not feel that way." It is better to let go of inner tension and frustration in a safe place than to internalize it and let it come to a point where the pressure causes an explosion, or where the anger comes out in damaging ways.

Living in our fast-moving society causes stress. There is job insecurity, financial troubles and disasters all around us. We cannot help but be affected by the suffering of humanity, whether it be close by or far away. As a chaplain, I am able to be with patients and clients in their pain, but when that pain comes too close because a loved one is in distress, it becomes my pain to such an extent that I also need support.

Stress, therefore, can be relieved by sharing it with a friend. If we can say to that friend, "I need to talk," and he or she is able to listen in a non-judgmental way, we have an advantage. When we put into words what is churning inside of us, we realize how angry or sad we really are. Expressing these feelings helps us to look at them and make a decision on how to deal with them. When given a chance to air their anger or frustrations, people often come around and say things like, "Oh, well, I guess I can bear with it," or "I just have to make the best of it." One patient's family member was bristling with anger at a situation in the hospital that caused him grief and inconvenience. He was going to write to administration to voice his complaint. When I said that I could understand how he felt angry and that he should write, he deflated considerably. Someone had understood and validated his feelings.

Even though not all that we say may be valid, it is a way of testing our own feelings when we can share them with a friend. Sometimes we can be that friend or sometimes we need that friend. Jesus is our friend, but most of the time we need someone who can convey those Christ-like qualities to us. As a chaplain, I am like a friend who listens, who encourages, who shares joys and sorrows, and who feels solidarity with those who are angry with unjust situations.

26

Joy and Sorrow

Blessed is the one who comes
in the name of the LORD.
Psalm 118:26a

*T*he question was asked if chaplains are only
present for people who experience trauma,
loss, grief or death. While it's true that chaplains are called mainly for occasions of grief or loss, they
also witness happy events.

I, who work in Obstetrics, drop in on new parents all
the time and see their delight over their newborn children. Often I hear the remark that babies and the
process of birth are miracles. Just before delivery, the
baby is still fully dependent on the mother for suste-
nance, but after birth, there is an independent little
human being, complete with ten fingers and toes, mov-
ing, breathing, sucking, crying and all the rest. It is
good to reflect on this with the parents while they are
still in this stage of newness. Together we may give
thanks to God for the safe arrival of a new family member and we can marvel at God's goodness. Other parents
may be more down to earth about the birth of a baby, or
they may not be in the mood to rejoice after surgery or
an exhausting labour, but birth and the miracle of a
baby is a joyful event nevertheless.

Other occasions that call for rejoicing are when an

operation has gone well, or when no cancer was found as was feared, or when there is cancer but the physician was able to get it all, or when cancer was found early so there is a good chance of recovery. I, as chaplain, can be joyful with them, although there is a serious undertone to this kind of thankfulness. The main thing is that together we can find things to be thankful for. Patients often say that there are good doctors, tests, procedures and treatments which may be seen as gifts from God to restore health or prolong life. The diagnosis of cancer does not necessarily mean the death sentence, and if patients feel very down, this can be brought to their attention. In other words, I may give them hope, always keeping in mind not to give false hope.

Often there is thankfulness when an elderly patient has passed into eternity after having lived a long and fruitful life. The bitter and sweet are mixed — there is the pain of the immediate loss, but also the joy of a life well-lived. Often old age comes with limitations and illness, and the families usually accept death as loss, but also as a release from suffering.

There is happiness when the pastoral care team gathers together with patients for worship or singing, or when we join them for a birthday party. In this time of serious cutbacks to the health care system, patient care is no longer the same. Yet patients and families are still thankful for doctors and nurses who make the best of the situation, and for volunteers who play an increasingly important role in caring for the sick, disabled and elderly.

It is amazing that no matter how trying the circumstances are, there is always something for which to be thankful. Often patients will say, "I am so much better off than this or that person." I try to bring out the good in a bad situation if the person is receptive to it; at other times I simply allow them to process bad news first since they are not yet ready to see some light.

I find satisfaction in being with others in times of joy and sorrow because I know that it is important to be with people when they need to express their emotions. All of us have gone through times of joy and sorrow, and we know how important it is to have someone with whom to share. As a chaplain, I come not only to be there personally, but I come in the name of the Lord to convey the presence and comfort of our God. The tools I carry with me are God's presence and Spirit, God's Word and prayer. Spiritual care is life-giving because it calls forth hope for life's needs, it conveys mercy, and it provides strength where there is weakness.

27
A Complete Bible

When you pass through the waters,
I will be with you; and through the rivers,
they shall not overwhelm you;
Isaiah 43:2a

*D*ull grief showed in her eyes; she had just miscarried a baby that she had been expecting for some months. I do not use the medical term "fetus" when I talk about this kind of loss because, to the parents, it is a baby — a child that is part of them. When I came to her bedside, she did not want to talk, but she did start crying. It took some time before she said, "It's probably for the better because I just left my husband and moved to this city." It was at that point that I asked if I could sit down to have a talk. I do not always know if my visits are welcome and, therefore, I have to wait for the right moment to start listening. Listening means giving feedback, trying to put myself into a situation. As we reflected together on her life, it became apparent that there had been much grief and pain in her marriage relationship. Her husband was unemployed and had become abusive, and Julie had had to leave him for her and her child's safety.

Julie struggled with guilt-feelings over against the Church and God. Was she so messed up that she could not even keep a marriage together, she asked herself. I pointed out that it takes two to keep a covenant, and it takes two to keep a marriage together. She talked and cried for an hour; it was one of those days when I saw many tears flow. All the pent-up grief seemed to come out. She was fortunate that she could stay with relatives who had offered to help. I read a passage for her from Isaiah 3 to give her comfort and hope.

When the hospital opened, one of the duties of the pastoral care department was to put a Gideon Bible in every nighttable. It was that Bible that was on Julie's bed when I came to visit the next day. She was ready to go home, but she had been trying to find the passage I had read to her, because it had comforted her. I noticed that she could not find Isaiah and she said she would find it at home. I asked her what kind of Bible she had at home and she said it was a New Testament. This gave me an opportunity to give her a complete Bible, with Isaiah in it. I pointed out that this Bible had an index in the front with headings for all situations in which people find themselves, such as grief, hope, despair, loneliness, etc. I also showed her the index for the Bible books and I marked Isaiah, the Psalms and the gospels. I asked her to pray first before she started reading so that the Spirit of God would guide her in her reading and make clear to her what she needed. I also gave her my card so that she could contact me if need be. She has not done so, so I leave her in the hands of God and pray that He will provide people for her who can surround her with love and practical help.

Every morning I pray that God will guide my work and lead me to those who need help most. I am sure that my prayer was heard that day because Julie was one of those who needed the comfort of God's love very much. One thing I can do for all the patients and family members I have been in contact with is pray for them. I do not remember them all by name, but it is comforting to know that God does and that I am only a very small part of God's involvement in people's lives.

28
Fear

"...do not be afraid, for I am with you...."
Genesis 26:24b

*M*y husband and I are fortunate that we live at the outskirts of a big city, so that we can walk or bike into the country. One sunny evening, I was walking past a pond and I had to chuckle at the sight of a red-headed woodpecker drilling into a telephone pole. Now that it is fall and the berries are ripening, I enjoy the saskatoons and I pick flowers to my heart's content. Even if I had no flowers around the house, I could pick enough wild flowers to fill my need for some colour and beauty around me. The mountain ash berries are turning red already and we are waiting for the waxwings to come and feast on them. I am gathering the seedpods of poppies and other plants so that I can work with dried flowers. I am always looking for what nature provides to beautify our home. Soon I can pick bright red crab apples to put in a basket and their fragrance will spread throughout the house.

As I was walking past the pond one evening, I watched a duck swim around with six ducklings following close behind. They swam seemingly effortlessly in the water, leaving barely a ripple. But I knew that underneath the surface, those little webbed feet were paddling very hard. I could not help but comparing this to people who on the surface seem calm and serene but underneath they may be in turmoil. Sometimes I wonder what the real feelings are underneath the calm faces. A nervous twitching of the hands or a trembling of the mouth may tell a different story than what people say. We often do the same when someone asks how we are doing; we say, "fine," when it may not be true at all. What bothers me is that some right away say, "How about yourself?" thereby diverting the attention away from themselves. This may be a way of avoiding sharing their feelings or problems with others.

Now that patients come through the hospital in rapid succession for short-stay surgeries, I try to see them in between admission and the time of surgery. Some are honest enough to say that they are nervous or that they'll be glad when it's over. Sometimes people ask for a prayer while others talk about their fear of the anesthesia. It is the loss of control they fear or of not waking up. Deep down there is a fear of death and I can understand that fear. I thought I had worked through the fear of dying when I was sick, but when, after surgery, my vital signs went down, I was very fearful. Certain experiences serve me well so that I can understand what others go through. If I detect fear, I offer to pray with patients or, if they are not comfortable with prayer, I just stay and talk or hold their hand and reassure them that God watches over them, that the doctors are competent and that the medical team keeps a close eye on the patients. Calm exteriors can hide anxiety or fear, but I also have to be careful not to try and detect fear if there is not any. Some people just have an inner peace and restfulness that is real because they know their life is in God's hand. Then we rejoice together. Others have an attitude of "whatever will be, will be."

Often when I walk in a mall and see so many people passing each other, I wonder what goes on under the mask of their faces. Some may be grieving or hurting from some deep wounds, while others may be worried about a loved one. Some may be full of anticipation of a joyful event. What do we really know of each other, even in the household of faith? I pray that in the faith family especially, we will learn to share more of our joys and sorrows. I am sure that God, our parent, would approve and rejoice if we could become more open and vulnerable so that we can not only comfort, but be comforted.

29
Spiritual Wellness

*You then, my child, be strong in the grace
that is in Christ Jesus;*
2 Timothy 2:1

One of the aspects of my work as a chaplain was to spend an hour every two weeks with a group of psychiatric outpatients. The focus of this group was spiritual wellness. I tried to initiate a conversation with these patients to help them express their thoughts and feelings and bring them out into the open for feedback from the other people. By revealing some of their thoughts, these patients would become more aware of what was on their minds and what their problems were. We discussed such things as their relationship to God, anger, hope, fear, whether religion was a help or a hindrance for them, what gave them strength, which people in their lives have encouraged them, and what their best and worst memories were.

Some days these discussions took off and patients started talking freely; other times they had difficulty thinking, let alone talking, because of medication or depression. I realized that we were treading on very fragile territory and the nurse who was present also assessed the responses to see if they might reveal some hidden aspects of the patients.

I approached these topics with caution, careful not

to offend, but to receive whatever was said without judgement or disapproval. I appreciated a straight-forward remark from the heart much more than a "trying to please the chaplain" approach. At times, a person would lash out at the Church because of hurts they felt they had received from either religious figures or clergy, or people who professed to be followers of Christ. The topic of forgiveness evoked much reaction; pure hatred sometimes came to the surface at the thought of having to forgive an abuser or offender. We then talked about the process of forgiveness, that it can take a long time and we have to be patient with ourselves.

The people in the group gave feedback to each other and that was helpful. Sometimes they accepted remarks from others better than from the treatment team. Anger at God was prevalent; it was easy to blame God when something went wrong. It was amazing how people who had no use for God were so ready to blame Him when their lives fell apart! For some, God did not exist anymore because He did not live up to their expectations. Sometimes people needed to be challenged on their assumptions and sometimes their anger just needed to be accepted. The mystery of suffering has and always will be with us and often an understanding approach did more to help the patient's search for meaning than an argument about the goodness of God, which would be dismissed immediately.

I, as a person of faith and hope, let myself become vulnerable at times, to make connections. To share of oneself is profoundly helpful in gaining trust, and I trust that by committing to God each and every one of those sessions, they were blessed. It released me of the burden to provide answers to the searching ones, and to allow them to find their own answers. I heard their stories and stayed in their space of bewilderment or anger, and in that space, I believed that the Spirit would do its work. I sometimes felt angry that God seemed so silent when people called out for help. Could there not be some sign of compassion or love? Then I realized that those of us who are able to be present to those in need may be the only presence of God that they will ever encounter — and that is an awesome thought!

30

Defeated

> *"Come to me, all you that are weary*
> *and are carrying heavy burdens,*
> *and I will give you rest."*
> Matthew 11:28

ebecca came in contact with me through a friend who was concerned about her. Rebecca was not her usual self after the loss of a baby and she had become depressed. As we sat down to talk, it became clear that it was not only this last loss that she was grieving for, but there were other losses in the past which she had not dealt with, as well. It turned out that Rebecca's professional endeavour was successful, but on the personal level, she was so lost that she needed help to sort out her life. She needed to look at her self, her values and her goals to see where she was headed.

Rebecca had not been able to maintain a steady relationship with a partner and she was left to do her grieving by herself. She had no direction, no goals, no faith in God to sustain her, and there was nothing left to give her the desire to live. She wanted meaning in her life — someone or something for which to live. That's why she had wanted a baby: to have someone to care for and love. Many teenagers want a baby for this reason; they feel a void in their lives and seek to fill it by having a sweet, cuddly baby. Little do they realize that giving birth to a child does not mean possessing him or her, but rather raising that child as a person in his or her own right, as a child of the Creator. Raising and loving children is a most difficult task because so much is at stake, and teenagers do not realize this. They romanticize motherhood.

Rebecca, however, had left the teenage years far behind and she came to find help in her search for meaning. I listened to a lovely person who was so emotionally empty because she had been dealt such hard blows in her life. Deaths and disappointments had come to such a point that she could not handle it anymore. She had had enough.

I could gather from Rebecca's stories that God is working in her life. God often works in the depths of despair when all else loses its meaning. The career she had worked so hard for was not life-giving anymore. What was once important was not anymore. Chances that she would ever have a family were diminishing. What was the sense of living, she wondered.

At the end of our time together, Rebecca asked for a Bible, although she needed some help reading it. I gave her a booklet with selected verses which were more helpful at this point. She also asked for prayer and I am sure that God honoured our prayer as the cry for help that it was. I tried to put into words for her the desire for a return of a sense of purpose and for a calm whereby she could commit her life to the Lord of life. Rebecca needs to learn to cast all her burdens on God, who is the only one who can give her rest. Once that rest comes, her outlook on life will take on a different dimension.

"But," she said, "how do I pray? I am not used to it, and I am not sure that God wants me. How do I know that my prayers do any good?"

It will take much practice for her to start lifting her burdens from her own shoulders onto God's. I myself often forget to do this, and take on problems myself. It takes trust to believe and keep on believing that God is in charge of our lives. Slowly, Rebecca will have to start believing that there is rest for her too, and renewed energy to go on with life. God did not promise us a problem-free life, but He did promise to walk with us. I am sure that Rebecca needs people to stand by her in her struggle against depression and feeling defeated. She wanted to come back to talk some more, but as yet, she has not. Rebecca, don't let go of the glimmer of hope you felt when we talked. God will not let you go; you just have to believe it and act on it.

31

Dreams

...but this one thing I [Paul] do: forgetting
what lies behind and straining forward
to what lies ahead,
I press on toward the goal for the prize of the
heavenly call of God in Jesus Christ.
Philippians 3:13b-14

*L*ately I have been thinking again of some dreams I had at the time I started on the road to the chaplaincy. These dreams were indicative of an inner struggle that went on in me at an unconscious level. I will share some of these dreams to make the reader aware that my decision to enter the ministry in the Christian Reformed denomination was not made lightly. This whole process caused great inner turmoil, the depth of which I was not even aware. This struggle took place on a deep spiritual and emotional level — it was a struggle to accept what I was about to become: a woman in ministry.

I had many dreams where I was in a dangerous situation and tried to run away but my feet would not move. These dreams were very vivid and frightening. In the daytime I could handle my inner conflict by being rational about it, but the anxiety I felt came out in those dreams. Another set of dreams were those that involved a suitcase. In one of those dreams, I was on a journey in my country of birth. I had to get off the train before I had reached my destination because my suitcase was missing. I remember walking through the cobbled streets and not being able to find my suitcase. Another dream that stands out is one where I found myself at a wide expanse of water like a strait in the coastal states of the United States. A woman was sitting in a tiny boat and inviting me to come for a boat ride, destination unknown. I got scared and said, "No, I cannot come, because I do not have my suitcase with me."

I have often wondered about the meaning of the suitcase that was always missing. Many years later, I had another dream. I was at an airport and was looking for my suitcase at the baggage counter. Someone said, "There it is," and pointed to one of those old-fashioned suitcases with reinforced corners. I said, "No way, that's not mine." "Well, open it," was the advice of the bystanders. And yes! There were my belongings, clothes and books. However, the suitcase was not mine. The outer shell did not go together with the contents.

I believe these dreams were significant because I remember them so clearly. At first, the suitcase was out there somewhere, not to be found. In the latest dream, I found a suitcase that did not belong to me but had my belongings in it. There was some progress. Earlier, I could not go on a trip or journey because I felt incomplete without my belongings, whatever they signified. I was not ready to take the step or ready to leave behind that part of myself that was a hindrance.

The trip on that wide sea arm looked very frightening, yet liberating and inviting. But I did not dare to venture out because I was still shackled to the past, signified by the suitcase. The latest dream was different in that I finally found a suitcase, but a strange one. I wonder: Was it that the outer shell did not fit the contents? Or does the strange suitcase signify ordination that belongs with the office of chaplain, but that is not mine? I am waiting for some more insight into the meaning of these dreams. Maybe sometime I will have a dream wherein I feel completely at home with my role as chaplain and wherein I also feel accepted by the Church. I wonder what kind of a suitcase I will carry around then and on what kind of a journey I will be. Maybe it will be my heavenly journey where everything will finally be in place and each and everyone will be completely acceptable regardless of gender or race.

Random Acts of Kindness

As God's chosen ones, holy and beloved,
clothe yourselves with compassion, kindness,
humility, meekness, and patience.
Colossians 3:12

*O*nce again I was reading the story of Jeremiah, in Jeremiah 38. Jeremiah told King Zedekiah that the people of Judah would be taken into captivity by the King of Babylon for breaking the covenant with Yahweh. King Zedekiah did not want to hear this and, being a coward, did not dare to go against the princes who suggested that Jeremiah be put to death. Consequently, Jeremiah was lowered into a cistern of mud and left to starve to death. However, he was rescued by an Ethiopian eunuch, Ebed-melech, who, at the king's orders, drew Jeremiah out of the pit and restored him to the court of the guard. Ebed-melech took worn-out clothes and rags and let them down into the cistern for Jeremiah to put these under his armpits before he was pulled up. Now that is showing kindness! God rewarded Ebed-melech for his kindness to the prophet and promised that he would not perish when disaster struck Jerusalem (Jer. 39:15-18).

This story brought to mind the phrase, "a random act of kindness" — not a biblical saying, but certainly a noble stance. Kindness is the mark of a Christian, as we are told to clothe ourselves with kindness, among other things. All of us have met people who are good, who do their duty, who do their work well, but who are not necessarily kind. Kindness means going that extra mile, doing that extra something, like holding a door open, letting someone into a line-up of cars, or sending a card. Doing small, insignificant things for others can become a lifestyle.

"Random" means "here and there, not expecting anything in return." Ebed-melech the Ethiopian did not know beforehand that Yahweh would reward him with safekeeping, yet he went the extra mile of providing those rags for Jeremiah to prevent the ropes from cutting into his flesh. Can you imagine being let down into a cistern, sinking into the mire and being left to starve to death? Prophets sure suffered for bringing God's judgment on people, and God let that happen.

In visiting the sick, I often hear the question, "Why does God let this happen?" Yet God allowed his messengers to suffer; many of the apostles met a cruel death. Could not God be a bit more rewarding for those who spread the good news? But if God did not spare them, why should He spare us? If we look at those whose lot is worse than ours, we'd be better off asking, "Why *not* me?" We do not understand God's ways and there comes a time when we just have to let God be God.

The consolation in all this is that God provides people to walk beside us and sustain us, if only through a random act of kindness. God may intervene directly in our lives, but more often, He works through people and through the prayers of people. We do not know what our kindness will mean, but it may restore a certain person's trust in humanity. Sometimes we need to be receivers of those acts of kindness and other times, the givers.

Through a random act of kindness, we may unknowingly be used of God to lighten someone's burden or to brighten someone's day. As followers of Christ, we should practice these acts of kindness, not to receive a reward, but out of commitment to the One who showed us the ultimate act of self-giving. The challenge is to be kind to those who are not kind to us, to not repay them for what they do or fail to do, but to just practice kindness.

33

Thanksgiving

You sweep them away; they are like a dream....
Psalm 90:5a

*T*he season of Thanksgiving brings to mind another Thanksgiving when I was on call. A young woman was brought into emergency having been involved in a motor vehicle accident. She was driving home to be with her extended family when the accident happened. The family lounge near the Intensive Care Unit became the gathering place for parents, brothers, sisters and other relatives as they gradually arrived to be together in the face of tragedy. Their grief and agony was hard to witness.

When the patient arrived in the hospital everything possible was done to revive her. She was connected to an artificial respirator on which she would stay until the doctors could determine whether there was any hope of recovery. A day went by and the family waited, too shocked to say much; some paced the hallways, some just stared into space. I sat with them off and on, asking if I could be of any help. But there was nothing anyone could do but wait; their anxiety and questions were not verbally expressed but their agony was very evident. Prayers were not voiced, but sorrowing hearts reached out for consolation and meaning.

Gradually, the realization that there was no hope

began to sink in. The doctor came with the agonizing question: Would the family consent to the donation of the patient's organs? Tests showed that their loved one was brain dead, but her body was intact. The chest heaved normally as the machine did its work, and it was very difficult to believe that the patient was not able to breathe on her own. So the idea of taking organs out of someone who looks to be alive was excruciating to think about and something which this family could not bring themselves to do. Other people may feel that something good will come out of an accidental death and someone else may get a new lease on life because of organ donation. I tried to help the family see this aspect — that they could help someone else — but they refused to consider it. No pressure whatsoever was put on the parents to make a decision in favour of donation, but the Hope team (the team that looks after transplants) was disappointed to see this opportunity slip away.

After talking with the family, the doctor finally disconnected the breathing machine. They gathered around the bed to witness the quiet passing on. I stayed with them during these agonizing moments, until the monitor indicated that life had ebbed away. Their leave-taking was done in silence, and my presence was also one of quietness, in response to their need. They left heartbroken as I accompanied them to the door.

Often this Thanksgiving event comes back to me at this time of the year and I think how this family must relive the tragic loss of a young woman in the prime of her life. God's ways are mysterious and we cannot fathom why these things happen. As we all are faced, or will be faced sometime, with seemingly senseless losses, we try and find meaning in these events, just as Job in the Bible did. Yet we know that God does not allow these things to happen as punishment, because that was removed through Jesus Christ's death. However, we do live in an imperfect world and the meaning of tragedies may forever remain hidden from us. For some people, tragic events cause them to re-evaluate their lives; for others, these events become a source of bitterness.

I pray that these loving, caring family members will be able to deal with their pain in such a way that it will not defeat them, but rather deepen them. I trust that my presence with them as a representative of God was able to help them face their loss. I pray that they may find solace in the love of God, and that they may experience God's love directly and through others reaching out to them.

34

Giving

For if the eagerness is there, the gift
is acceptable according to what one has —
not according to what one does not have.
2 Corinthians 8:12

Reformed people are great givers for all kinds of causes. The Calvinist ethos is undoubtedly at the heart of this, encouraging such things as commitment, a sense of duty and a dedication to extending a helping hand in word and deed. We, as Reformed people, also want to make sure that our donated money goes where it is most needed. In our dedication to give to causes such as Hunger Fund and Disaster Relief, etc., we may overlook a need that is closer to home.

This brings to mind a clothing drive a church once conducted. Boxes were rapidly filling up with good quality clothes to be given to a downtown centre for the needy and homeless. It so happened that a man from the street walked into the church with two bags and helped himself to some warm clothes. Needless to say, this upset the people who were in charge of the drive, and I reflected on the incident. If this man was needy — and indeed he must have been — he was helped by having some warm clothes to wear. It was, of course, the fact that he did not ask for permission that rankled the church workers. But did it really matter? Maybe he was too embarrassed to ask.

Another drive is being conducted annually in the hospital chapel. An undecorated Christmas tree is placed in the chapel and over time, the branches are decorated with hats, mittens, slippers, socks and scarves, donated by staff and patients. These collected items are then donated to a worthy cause by Christmas time. The chapel is open for anyone who wants to come and spend some time in prayer or meditation. One day, we found a note from someone who had taken a pair of warm socks from the tree because her feet were cold. Another patient asked for some slippers for her kids and these were gladly given. In this way, we could fill a need close to home. We need to keep this in mind with all of our giving. Our giving becomes more rewarding when we know who the recipient is. The pictures of starving people across the ocean haunt us, and doing something for one or more of these children puts a face to suffering and makes us feel more connected. May our eyes and hearts be open to the needs around us, close by and far away.

Giving does not only happen in the form of dollars and cents, of course, but also in the form of time, effort and commitment. For those who are retired and living on a reduced income, donation may come in a different way. Where monetary giving may decrease, other kinds of giving can increase. Families with limited resources may have to find other ways to help out others; it can be done in many ways. Each one of us needs to determine what our gifts are and where they can best be directed to serve God in this world.

35

Where Have All the Women Gone?

For freedom Christ has set us free.
Galatians 5:1a

question that was put to me by a patient started me thinking again about relationships between men and women in relation to God and other believers. The question this patient asked was if she was correct in saying that the Trinity consisted of God the Father, the Virgin Mary and Jesus. I explained to her what the traditional view of the Trinity was, of course, but I realized that this patient needed to have a woman in the Trinity for her to understand who God was.

The doctrine of the Trinity, consisting of God the Father, God the Son and God the Holy Spirit, has contributed to the belief that God is exclusively male. It took centuries for this doctrine to reach its final form as we know it and this long process shows that this doctrine was formulated by men who were bound by their time and place in history and by their understanding of God. This doctrine came out of a patriarchal view of humankind. In biblical times, under the patriarchal system, the man was seen as directly under God, then

women, children, slaves, etc. In the Ten Command-
ments for instance, we read the command, *You shall not
covet your neighbour's house; you shall not covet your
neighbour's wife, or male or female slave, or ox, or don-
key, or anything that belongs to your neighbour* (Exod.
20:17). The neighbour's wife fell in the same category as
the slave or ox as possessions of the husband. Nowa-
days we do not believe that this last commandment was
only meant for men; already we have come a long way
in recognizing that the New Testament is teaching us a
different way.

A theologian once said that history is the process by
which we come to self-understanding, and I believe that
God's Spirit enlightens our minds. Humankind has
slowly come to the understanding that slavery was
wrong, although the Bible does not forbid it. Not very
long ago, apartheid was abolished because people could
no longer believe that apartheid, based on racism, was
justified. Now that we are at the end of the twentieth
century, men and women come to realize that inequality based on gender is not acceptable anymore and that
it is a matter of injustice. The Church, as the body of
Christ, has the example of Jesus who treated women as
persons in their own right, women who did not need
men as intermediaries between them and God. Many
believers find it hard to accept that freedom in Jesus
Christ, and to grant women equal status with men is
still very threatening, especially where women in official ministry is concerned. The argument has been used
that Jesus appointed only male disciples, but as far as
we know, Jesus did not have disciples of colour either.
Are we then going to say that black people cannot be

disciples, or cannot be ordained?

Men as representatives of God are still often thought to be the only ones who can carry out the task of official ministry, even though both women and men were created in the image of God. I realize that we are not just going to change age-old doctrines, but we do need to re-examine them. New formulations of what we believe have become necessary. The Christian Reformed Church, for instance, has written a contemporary testimony to help us relate in contemporary terms to the Word of God. Therefore, it would be helpful to look at the doctrine of the Trinity again and to think of God in terms of a spirit, whom we may see as a father and as a mother. God says in Isaiah 66:13, *As a mother comforts her child, so I will comfort you*; and in Isaiah 42:14, *For a long time I have held my peace, I have kept still and restrained myself; now I will cry out like a woman in labour, I will gasp and pant.* There are many more passages where God is portrayed as a woman or mother. All the metaphors used for God are to help us in our human understanding of who God is, and the metaphors of God as female have not been given enough attention. Seeing God as male and female and knowing that we are created in that image would change how we relate to each other as believers and co-workers in God's Kingdom.

According to the genealogies in the Bible, the men seemed to have begotten their offspring all by themselves. The women were not worth mentioning. There are a few exceptions in Matthew 1, where Tamar, Rahab, Ruth, the wife of Uriah and Mary are mentioned. I, as one who has given birth and who is keenly aware of the process of birth and who hears the cries of women giving birth, often think of the pain experienced before and after giving life, and I think that women were not given their due in the Bible. This still carries over into the Church, the body of Christ. However, through the Holy Spirit, we have come to the understanding that we live under a different order — the order of redeemed relationships through the grace of God and the sacrifice of Jesus.

Christ has set us free for freedom — freedom to relate, accept and value each other as co-heirs with Christ, and that means both genders, one not more than another. Man (in the Dutch language the word "mens" is used to include both genders) was created in the image of God, *male and female He created them* (Gen. 1:27). The fall into sin happened, but its results have been redeemed by the blood of Christ. Both men and women have been restored to friendship with Christ. Women keenly feel that holding on to the old order is an injustice to their God-imaged womanhood, but this happens again and again when they are not considered equal partners in the gospel. I pray for the day that women will be welcomed with joy and open arms if they are called to the ministry of the Word and Sacraments.

36
Counting Our Days

*So teach us to count our days that we
may gain a wise heart.*
Psalm 90:12

It is a beautiful fall evening, the air is still and warm. The flowers are at their peak since we have had much rain and cool weather. These warm days are an unexpected gift after a cool summer and it makes saying farewell to the pleasures of summer a bit easier. Especially in a climate like ours (53° North), we have to make the most of the summer season before the snow flies. Making the most of what we have is a God-given task as well. We are not to live with a reckless motto of "eat, drink and be merry, for tomorrow we die." Rather, we are to value what the day brings and enjoy it while we can.

As our two mothers are reaching a ripe old age and are continually faced with more and more restrictions and losses, Job and I are reminded to make the most of our lives while we are able and healthy. These mothers, once healthy and strong, cared for their families during the depression years, the war and immigration. They worked hard and their capable hands guided and cared with dedication. Now those hands are resting and have lost their strength. Their minds are now turning inward towards those things that concern their immediate needs, and their world has become very small.

How did they gain a heart of wisdom, and what does that wisdom consist of, I wonder. Earthly goods lose their appeal for the elderly and interest in others wanes. They become more and more oblivious to the world around them and issues lose their importance. As one man on his deathbed once said to me, "All these issues in the Church don't really matter; now it is just God and me." Just God and me — as the end product of a fruitful life. Not everyone comes to that conclusion, but fortunate are those who do.

Of course, we need the promoters of justice and the fighters of worthwhile causes. Throughout history, there were people who were on fire for causes; the prophets of biblical times put their hearts and souls into their God-given tasks. The apostles paid with their lives for the cause of proclaiming Jesus Christ crucified. Of course, we need the dedicated people who keep families and churches going. Men and women to whom God has given burning hearts for a special ministry or project are given the energy to carry out that work.

Yet there is a time for everything — a time to work hard, a time to rest from it and a time to ask God to bless the work of our hands. What do we learn from those who have gained a wise heart? As I look back on the years of raising a family and the years in ministry, I gain perspective. I know that in the end, those things that are so important at a given time, fade away to make room for things eternal.

I had an inkling of that insight when I was told I had cancer. I experienced God's love through caring people in a special way that I had not felt before. I realized how much I was loved and how much I loved my husband, children, grandchildren, parents, brothers, sisters and friends. So many of them are part of my life and being. Life itself became so much more precious. I keep reminding myself of that awareness when it gets clouded over by the cares and concerns of living in an imperfect world.

What really counts is that I have lived my life in the best way I knew how, and that I have answered the call of God in my life. I ask God to forgive me for my fumbling efforts and for the damage I have done, but I also know that God will honour my faith and my sincerity and He will bless what I have done. And I too will gain a heart of wisdom and the discernment to know the difference between what is really important and what is not.

We Are Jesus' Friends

You are my friends if you do what I command you.
I do not call you servants any longer,
because the servant does not know what the master
is doing; but I have called you friends,
because I have made known to you everything
that I have heard from my Father.
John 15:14-15

We, the followers of Christ, have become Jesus' friends through the grace and Spirit of God. We have been redeemed from a state of servanthood to the stature of friends of Jesus. It is up to us to claim that status. As friends of Jesus Christ, we share in His suffering and in His glory, and we are entitled to the same power that was used to raise Jesus from the dead.

What do we do with this awareness? How do we know and see and feel that friendship? All of us, to some extent, by living in an era where most everything can be explained, have lost the capacity for wonder, awe and experiencing miracles. We have become skeptics. Richard Mouw in his book, *Consulting the Faithful,* says that all of us have some deep spiritual yearning and desire for visible and practical signs of God's presence in ordinary life.[3] There is an increased hunger for spiritual experiences in our day and age because, even with all the scientific facts and explanations, there is an emptiness that needs to be filled. We live in an age of immense unpredictability, change and insecurity. Consequently, there is a general trend from the outer experience to the inner, and people have begun paying more attention to mystery, imagination, connection with nature, etc. Of course, there all kinds of movements that try to fill these needs apart from Christianity. It is therefore important to keep our eyes on Jesus, the perfecter of our faith, who is the way, the truth and the life (John 14.6).

Jesus as our friend has given us the eyes of faith, and with those eyes of faith, we perceive and see things in ordinary life that are not so ordinary anymore. And with those eyes of faith, we come to see those visible and practical signs of God's presence. I have seen signs of these graced moments in patients as they go through fearful times. When I read a Scripture verse to them or say a prayer, it has special meaning because they are much more open to it than when life is going smoothly. It is exactly in our vulnerable moments that God speaks to us in special ways.

Psalm 23 is a special comfort to many, and I have always taken comfort in verse 3 where it says, *He [God] restores my soul*. Whenever I feel wounded, hurt or weary, it helps me to repeat that to myself. Just recently, I read again, "You shall lack nothing." It does not say, "You shall *have everything*"; no, "You shall *lack nothing*." To me, that means I shall have courage, strength, energy and whatever else I may need when I need it.

One of my friends once told the story of her seven-year old son. One of his little classmates had died and, as parents do, they told him that little Marietje was now in heaven with Jesus. One rainy day, the boy was sitting by the window looking at the sky, watching the clouds being blown by the wind. All at once, the sun came through and he sat there looking and looking in wonder. Then he ran to his mother excitedly and said, "Mom, I just saw Marietje's face and she was smiling at me!" In the lightness amid the clouds, this little boy's life was given a lift, because he had seen the face of his little friend. That was a graced moment. Some people have seen the face of Jesus or an angel.

Corrie ten Boom, author of *Each New Day*, was taken to a concentration camp during World War II for their family's involvement in hiding Jews from the Nazis. Corrie writes this story:

"Once while we were on roll call, a cruel guard kept us standing for a long, long time. Suddenly a skylark began to sing in the sky and all the prisoners looked up to listen to that bird's song. As I looked at the bird, I saw the sky and I thought of Psalm 103:11. O love of God, how deep and great, far deeper than a person's deepest hate. God sent that skylark daily for three weeks, exactly during roll call, to turn our eyes away from the cruelty of people to the ocean of his love."[4]

Corrie and the other prisoners, with their ears of faith, did hear the skylark's song as a sign of God's grace, and it gave them hope and courage to go on.

I believe that Jesus, as our friend, opens our spiritual eyes to signs of His grace. When my father died, I put his picture in a frame and I wrote underneath, *And I give them eternal life*, from the gospel of John. I had read that passage many times before, but in my grief, that verse became a special comfort. It would be helpful if someday we took the time to write down or share with others those graced moments God has given us, just so that we may draw strength from them time and again. God still speaks to us through words, nature, songs, Scripture and other people. When looking at the northern lights one night, I was awed by the majesty of God's creation, and my worries took on a different dimension. These worries were so insignificant compared to the majesty that was put on display that night. Thank you, God, for those graced moments, as a sign of Your friendship. Jesus' friendship can do for us what earthly friends cannot do. Thanks again, God, for opening our hearts and eyes to the wonder of Your friendship through Your son, Jesus, who calls us His friends.

[3]Richard J. Mouw, *Consulting the Faithful* (Grand Rapids: Wm. B. Eerdmans Publishing Co., 1994) p. 16.

[4]Corrie ten Boom, *Each New Day* (Minneapolis: World Wide Publications, 1977) January 25.

38

Darkness

For our struggle is not against enemies of blood and flesh, but against... the spiritual forces of evil in the heavenly places.
Ephesians 6:12

*H*alloween is more and more becoming an occasion for ghosts, witches, skeletons and skulls to come out of the woodwork. Television offers a variety of horror movies to match the season. Way back when our children went "Trick or Treating," it was a much more innocent event of dressing up and going to collect candy from door to door, than the present trend with the display of ghostly figures. "Hallowed evening" was a festival celebrated on October 31, the day before All Saint's Day. Traditionally, the Druids, an ancient order of Celtic priests in Northern Europe, believed that ghosts, spirits, witches, etc. came out to harm people at the time of this festival. The pranks that are played on people re-enact the harmful tricks these spirits allegedly played on their neighbours. The Roman Catholic Church declared November 1 as All Saint's Day in the 700's to honour all the saints, and the two festivals were combined into the Halloween festival.[5] The declaration of All Saint's Day was possibly an attempt by the Church to counteract these pagan customs, although the belief in druids, ghosts, etc. was still strong until the scientific age.

Whereas Halloween may be a fun time for youngsters to go from door to door for tricks and treats, or for others to have dress-up parties, I do not feel comfortable with the recent trend of ghosts and skeletons floating around. The display of anything that personates evil forces gives credence to these forces and even celebrates them. Evil is still with us and will be until Christ returns, but we do not have to pay so much attention to it, as if it were a joke or something to celebrate.

I was reminded of the presence of evil forces on Halloween when some people got into the hospital chapel and unscrewed lightbulbs and removed the crucifix. There we were confronted with spiritual forces that did not want to see light, but preferred darkness. The symbol of Jesus' suffering was removed. That was a sobering reminder of the forces of darkness right in our midst. People disturbing the chapel where others come to pray and connect with God was not a prank, but a deliberate act of defiance against Christianity.

This event was a reminder that Halloween is not an innocent festival, but a spiritual battle against forces of evil that are at work, *especially* on Halloween night. I for one have become very cautious on Halloween and pray for protection, that the light of God's presence will overcome the darkness, right here in the twentieth century. I also pray that we as Christ's followers may be walking testimonies of that light, and not give in to the darkness that is all around us, especially on Halloween when it manifests itself in a very public way.

---

[5]"Halloween," *World Book Encyclopedia*, 1967 ed.

39
Memorial Services

*You will not forget your misery; you will
remember it as waters that have passed away.*
Job 11:16

ragedies are hard to take for all concerned and they are part of the work of a chaplain in an active treatment hospital. It is difficult sometimes not to be able to follow up and walk some more with the people whom I have met under such trying circumstances. I recall, in particular, a camping and drowning accident, which involved deaths and a number of suicides. The question always arises if these accidents could have been avoided. How does one ever overcome such tragedies? I have had instances where, during the child-rearing years, accidents almost happened because of my not watching closely enough. These incidents still come back to haunt me and I thank God that our children were spared. Consequently, I can relate to those people who are not only dealing with grief and loss, but also with feelings of guilt and regret.

The short contact we as chaplains have with these families does not seem enough, but we have to trust that others after us will provide for their spiritual and emotional needs. Therefore, we are glad when the family's pastor is called and arrives to take over and carry on the supportive work once the family goes home. When people have no church connection, other family members or friends take over. Sometimes the chaplain is called on again to conduct a memorial service or to provide further support. Now that our hospital has become a Community Health Centre, one of our tasks is to provide more follow-up. However, the serious accidents and trauma cases will not come to our hospital anymore.

One avenue of carrying on the support is to provide memorial services, which we hold on a regular basis. The family members are invited to these services and the names of those who have died in the hospital are read or shown on a screen. One of the chaplains gives a comforting message and reading from Scripture. These services are well-attended and, afterwards, the chaplains connect again with the families. Some chaplains have spent a long time with a dying patient, for some it was just a short encounter when the patient was brought into emergency. Some we get to know better than others, but the encounters, however short, stay with people because it was meaningful for them. So after the memorial service we talk again and recall how it was, how it all went and how they are trying to carry on without that loved one. One man showed a picture of his young child, which he cried over when we talked. This remembering is an important part of the grieving process, especially if it is done in a supportive environment.

Some people come back for grief counselling or they are referred to a bereavement group. I had the privilege of visiting a mother who had given birth to a healthy baby after she and her husband had suffered the loss of a baby the year before. That was a happy follow-up, whereby the grief made way for joy. All in all, these involvements are usually short, but I trust God to provide for these people. Some have touched me in a special way and I will not forget them. They are stored in my memory and I somehow feel that my remembering them and lifting them up to God's mercy is a way of carrying them through, although they may not realize it. Even as God says, "I will not forget you," I, in my imperfection, will not forget these people whom I have met under such trying circumstances. I hope and pray that they have been helped by this ministry and that they are able to live with their losses and find happiness again.

40
Playfulness

They the ransomed of the LORD
shall return, and come to Zion with singing;
everlasting joy shall be upon their heads; they
shall obtain joy and gladness,
and sorrow and sighing shall flee away.
Isaiah 35:10

The children in our street are busy riding their bikes and skateboards. It is a beautiful summer evening but fall is in the air. Fall has come early, since our summer was cool and damp. With our long winters, we depend on summers to renew our energy and give us a chance to soak up the sunshine. It is with sadness that we are forced to say goodbye to hoped-for, sun-filled days, sitting on the deck and simply being outside. It hardly happened this summer and we are still hoping for a nice fall season.

The winter season has its own charm, with long evenings by the fireplace and the splendor of fresh snow on the trees and fields, but with it also comes a feeling of confinement. Sometimes the roads are too slippery to walk on and, since we have never been very sports-minded, we usually don't make the most of what winter has to offer. Driving on icy roads makes winter a less desirable time of year for elderly people. When our children longed for the snow to fall, we were quite willing to put it off. Who wants snow in October?

Hearing the children play brings back memories of long summer evenings when I played outside. But I also remember the very cold and snowy winter of 1944/45, which caused hardship due to lack of food and fuel. One particularly beautiful scenery I remember was a park where my mother and I went to gather up branches for the fireplace during this hunger winter. It was a private estate and I still remember the fear I felt of getting caught, but more than that, I marvelled at the beauty of the white frost on the trees and shrubs. Later on in time, I, with a group of children, went to that same park to beg a cigarette from the German soldiers who had taken up residence there. My father was not pleased, although he did crave to have a smoke. I never found out what he did with that cigarette.

My childhood was not filled with playfulness. I do remember spending time in nature, gathering up flower petals to make perfume and frog eggs to hatch. Sometimes I took flowers home, red poppies that only lasted one day in a jar. I cannot remember playing with dolls or teddybears; these were simply not part of our household at that time. The war took away from us much of what children are now so used to that they do not appreciate it. No wonder I had to re-learn how to be playful. But how does an adult play?

After the years of my depression, one of the gifts I thankfully received was the ability to feel joy again. Joy for the little things in life, gifts such as a beautiful sunset, walking in the rain, sweetpeas, a bowl of fresh potpourri and the smell of baking bread. Playing, however, is still difficult, but even allowing myself to do some craft, to make small Christmas gifts for our guests is a beginning. I can find pleasure in decorating our living space for Christmas and sharing it with family and friends, or just sitting with a small child who is content being watched by loving adults. I envy a child's capacity for joy. Their minds and personalities are not cluttered yet with problems and obligations. How I wish I was a child sometimes, then I would not have to re-learn the art of playfulness.

However, being a child does not necessarily equal happiness. Inner happiness is to have a spirit of contentment and a life lived to the fullest, with integrity, in response to God's invitation to rest in God's grace. I am thankful that I again can feel a child-like joy at some small thing and it tells me that I am learning to play again. I need that so much as an antidote to the illness and death that is part of my routine.

41

Burning Hearts

They [Cleopas and his wife] said to each other,
"Were not our hearts burning within us while
he [Jesus] talked to us on the road,
while he was opening the Scriptures to us?"
Luke 24:32

n this final chapter, I am using the story of Jesus walking with the people on the road to Emmaus as an example of what pastoral care is.* Jesus responded to the spiritual need of this couple as they searched for the meaning of the crucifixion and the resurrection. He entered into their world of thinking and was thereby treading on sacred ground. Jesus let them work out their own search and let them discover God's action in their lives. He called forth their strength and insight without revealing Himself to them immediately, thereby letting them come to their own conclusions. Yet He showed compassion and patience while they were trying to come to terms with the bewildering happenings in their lives. This couple had been deeply involved in Jesus' life and death as we know from John 19:25, where it says that Mary, the wife of Clopas (or Cleopas), had been near the cross of Jesus, together with his mother, his mother's sister and Mary of Magdala.

Cleopas and Mary were recalling all the events of

the past few days. They were still in the grieving stage, whereby they needed to go over all that had happened. They had enough time to talk at length during this seven-mile walk from Jerusalem to Emmaus. They had heard that Jesus was alive, but he had not yet been seen by anyone; they had only heard that some women has seen a vision of angels who said that Jesus was alive. So the joy of the resurrection was not there yet, and they were grieving the loss of their master and friend. Their faces were downcast.

When Jesus joined them, they felt a special presence as He walked with them and listened to them. He listened as they related the story of His death and how their expectations of a redeemer of Israel were shattered. They tried to make sense out of this chain of events, but they felt let down. Jesus let them experience their losses, not only of the death of a friend, but also of their hopes and expectations for a Messiah who was to liberate the nation of Israel. They were disillusioned.

Jesus, after having heard their story, started explaining why the Christ had to suffer. He connected with their suffering and identified with them in their search for answers. He explained that their perception of the Messiah was not the right one and that they needed to understand that Christ's suffering was necessary and that the prophecies had now been fulfilled. Jesus used the Jewish Scriptures, the books of Moses and the prophets, which no doubt were familiar to them. They heard the words that they knew so well and they started to understand. They felt comforted and it was at that point that their hearts started burning within them. They were not alone in their grief anymore, and in their greatest loss, they found comfort. It was Jesus' patient re-telling of the story that broke through their blindness and made them see the light.

The three of them went on and, as they approached their home, Jesus waited to be invited for supper because it was evening. As they were at the table, Jesus took the bread and gave thanks, broke it and gave it to them. We don't know if they were present at the last supper, but if they were, this may have reminded them of that night when He broke the bread. Through the breaking of the bread, they all of a sudden recognized Jesus and were filled with joy. Jesus, no doubt, explained to them that the breaking of the bread had become the symbol of the sacrificial giving of His body.

Then Jesus disappeared. I, for one, felt disappointment at this disappearance. Would it not have been better to be able to enjoy Jesus' company a little while longer, to let it all sink in and experience the relief of Jesus resurrection? Not so. Jesus left them and this couple immediately returned to Jerusalem, another seven miles! This time they were full of energy and eager to go and tell the good news. They had to share it and the sooner the better. The Scriptures had been fulfilled in a different way than they had expected, but now they understood!

They did not feel sadness anymore, because they had Jesus' presence in their hearts, as the burning in their hearts indicated, and now they went to share this presence with the others, with the community of faith. Jesus was still present in spirit and that gave them new hope. As they shared in His suffering, so they now shared in His resurrection. They were filled with renewed faith because their eyes had been opened to the real meaning of His death and resurrection.

Jesus walked with them not only literally, but more importantly, emotionally on their spiritual journey by listening to their story, and by allowing them their grief and bewilderment. He did not take away their suffering by saying, "Here I am, it's over." They needed to first understand why His death was necessary. By breaking through their perceptions, and by patiently explaining how it really was — "I needed to suffer" — they came to understand what the real meaning was and that their expectations were wrong.

In the breaking of the bread, a symbol of His suffering and resurrection, they recognized Him and they remembered. What a revelation! And this all happened because of Jesus' quiet presence. That is what pastoral caring is: walking with people, allowing them their grief and questions; sitting with them while they ask these questions; and showing compassion and identifying with their struggles. It is not rushing in with answers that may not even be their answers. People have to come to their own conclusions in their search for meaning. As chaplains, we can open the Scriptures to them, or, if people are not familiar with the Scriptures as the couple on the road to Emmaus were, the Spirit of the Scriptures may be conveyed in different ways. It may simply be a compassionate presence.

Chaplains allow the questions to come, though they may only be asked in silence. And when words come — hesitantly, slowly, expressing their searching — chaplains invite these words to come, not rushing them, after the example of Jesus on the road to Emmaus. Our wish is that, in shared faith, we may be able to break bread together, remembering that Jesus walked the *via dolorosa*, that He still identifies with all of our suffering, but that He is also the victor over death. For some, these trying times may lead to belief in Him who is the Resurrection and the Life. Many who know Jesus as the resurrected One draw strength from their faith in Him. For some, that belief may never come, but I for one continue to pray for all those with whom I have been in contact. I look forward to the day when everything will be made new, and I wonder if I will meet some of the people I have accompanied on their journeys. I know that on that day their sorrow will be changed to gladness and joy — and that keeps me going.

---

*I am indebted for some of these insights to Henri Nouwen, who held a speech on this passage.

Bibliography

"Halloween." *World Book Encyclopedia.* 1967 ed.

Johnson, B. Campbell. *Pastoral Spirituality.* Philadelphia: The Westminster Press, 1988.

Mouw, Richard J. *Consulting the Faithful.* Grand Rapids: Wm. B. Eerdmans Publishing Co., 1994.

ten Boom, Corrie. *Each New Day.* Minneapolis: World Wide Publications, 1977.

The following books are currently available from Essence Publishing:

Setting the Captives Free by John Visser ***106pp, $9.95***
Practical and biblical help in learning how we can be effectively used of God to make a difference in a hurting world. Includes Study Guide. Excellent for group study!

To Have and To Hold by John Visser. . . . . ***99 pp, $7.50***
Biblical Reflections on Marriage. Chapters include: God's Idea of Marriage; Living Happily Ever After; So, You're Single; Divorce & Remarriage; and more. Includes Study Guide. Excellent for Marriage Preparation Classes and married couples seeking to improve the quality of their marriage.

A Voice Behind You by Sheila White . . . . ***112 pp, $9.95***
This is a prophetic word to the Church by an anointed woman of God. It examines the present state of the Church and calls her towards her full destiny in Christ.

Handling Stress by John Visser . . . . ***112 pp, $9.95***
To live is to experience stress. Some people cope very well with stress while others do not. This book discusses causes and symptoms of stress in today's world and gives practical advice on how to handle it.

And the Pink Snow Fell by Rev. Ray Cross . . . ***100 pp, $14.95***
This is the story of the Port Hope, ON, gas explosion of November 1993 and the huge impact it had on one of the families living adjacent to the site of the explosion. Contains many photographs. Excellent for grief therapy!

Protestant Church Growth in Korea by Dr. John Kim . ***364 pp, $39.99***
The Korean Church is one of the fastest growing churches in the world today. In this book, the author offers some insights into why this is so and examines some of the factors that have influenced this growth.

A Lift for Living by Herman Kroeker . . . . ***363 pp, $16.95***
A daily devotional for the whole year by a veteran servant of God. Excellent for gift-giving and personal use.

*For more information or to place an order,
please contact your local Christian Bookstore
or:*

103B Cannifton Road
Belleville, ON K8N 4V2

*Phone (613) 962-3294; Fax (613) 962-3055
1-800-238-6376*

*A convenient Order Form is available on
the next page.*

Order Form

Ordered By: (please print)

Name: _____

Address: _____

City: _____ Prov./State: _____

Postal/Zip Code: _____ Telephone: _____

Please send me the following book(s): (All Prices in Cdn. Dollars.)

Qty.	Title	Unit Price	Total
_____	*Binder of Wounds*	$11.95	$_____
_____	*Setting the Captives Free*	$9.95	$_____
_____	*To Have & To Hold*	$7.50	$_____
_____	*A Voice Behind You*	$9.95	$_____
_____	*Handling Stress*	$9.95	$_____
_____	*And the Pink Snow Fell*	$14.95	$_____
_____	*Protestant Church Growth in Korea*	$39.95	$_____
_____	*A Lift for Living*	$16.95	$_____

Shipping ($3.00 first book - $1.00 each add. book): $_____

G.S.T. @ 7%: $_____

Total: $_____

Payable by Cheque, Money Order or [VISA]

VISA #:_____ Expiry:_____

Signature:_____

**To order by phone, call our toll-free number,
1-800-238-6376
and have your credit card handy.**